Magic of Believing

Torrie:
May you be blessed
with treasures of joy!
Leo Andrus
3·23·01

Dragonhawk Publishing Titles

Young Person's School of Magic and Mystery

VOLUME I:

Magic of Believing

by

Ted Andrews

DRAGONHAWK PUBLISHING   JACKSON, TENNESSEE

A DRAGONHAWK PUBLISHING BOOK

Magic of Believing

(Volume I of *Young Person's School of Magic and Mystery*)
Text and cover copyright ©2000 by Ted Andrews
Etching images copyright ©2000 by Diane Haugen

First Edition

Editing and indexing by Pagyn Alexander

Book design and layout by Diane Haugen
(http://www.wcdd.com/index.html)

ISBN 1-888767-43-X

Library of Congress Catalog Card Number: 00-100043

This book was designed and produced by

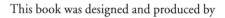

Dragonhawk Publishing
Jackson, Tennessee
USA

Dedication

For Theresa
and her wonderful new adventure!

Table of Contents

MAGICAL PRACTICES
(Exercises)

Preface

A Word to Parents and Students

The world truly is a place of great magic, mystery, and wonder. No group of people is more aware of this than our children. They know the rustling of leaves is a kind of whisper and wishing upon a star has great power. They know there really are ghosts and spirits and that their dreams are glimpses into other worlds and possibilities.

Young people have a great interest in the mystical, the psychic, and the magical, but much of what they know has come to them distorted by movies and television or complicated through confusing books that often are written in clouded, adult "New Age-speak." Too often the psychic and magical world becomes a place of fear and doubts rather than a place of wonder and enchantment. Without meeting their unique learning needs and skill levels, or without the right guidance and encouragement, the magic in the child disappears.

From preschoolers to teenagers and college students, interest in the psychic, the spiritual, and the magical is exploding. Parents are more aware than ever that their children are seeing auras, speaking of past lives, and experiencing spirit. Many of our young people are demonstrating healing touch or having prophetic dreams. And yet little has ever been created to encourage this interest or to help develop these skills within the young. What is most often missing is a way of helping them understand and work with their magical abilities and intuitive energies.

Although there has always been a great deal of material available for general development of psychic abilities, most of the materials and techniques are not designed to meet the unique needs of young people. Generally what has been written is for adults, and while some of it may be applicable to young people, a great deal of the material is not suitable for them (and sometimes not even for the adults themselves). Determining what is suitable can be difficult for those who are experienced. For the young and inexperienced, it is nearly impossible.

The creation of the YOUNG PERSON'S SCHOOL OF MAGIC AND MYSTERY resolves this problem. Great care has been taken to develop a unique course of study which can be beneficial and enjoyable for the young person wishing to unfold his or her own inner magic. It will also benefit the inexperienced and young-at-heart adult explorer as well.

To make this even more possible, we have gathered a faculty of delightful and skilled teachers to develop this course of study to guide the young seeker into new realms of possibilities. All are extremely knowledgeable and experienced in teaching both the young and adults. They are experts in their areas of study, and they can demonstrate all they teach. They live the magical life.

As we began to look more closely at all of them, we found they have other unique qualities in common. All of our teachers are well rounded in their education and experience. They are all practical and grounded, and they have a contagious enthusiasm about their work and their life. And most importantly, they have both a sense of responsibility and a sense of humor about themselves, about the world, and especially about the magical life.

Our teachers provide techniques which are safe and productive. Their methods, exercises, and games are intended to develop, entertain, and affirm the magic that exists in us all. Each course in the school supports and adds to what comes before or follows. Through this study, young people who feel "different" will become more accepting of their unique gifts. Their inner gifts will blossom throughout life and the creative contributions of these young people to the adult world in the new millenium will go well beyond what we can imagine!

We have chosen an initial ten subjects, although others will be added in time. We believe these provide a strong foundation for the student and will lay the groundwork for future, in-depth magical development. However, we will not be learning about casting spells or turning enemies into toads. This school is about helping young people find their inner magic and developing it over a lifetime.

If you provide the right teachers with the right methods, the magic will unfold. While many of us as children had to ignore, fear, or hide our special experiences, today's young people can now embrace and understand these happenings. Their experiences can become invitations to a life of great magic and wonder.

For parents, the YOUNG PERSON'S SCHOOL OF MAGIC AND MYSTERY provides a wonderful opportunity to explore spiritual mysteries with their children. This series provides guidance for working effectively with young people exploring what adults were often never encouraged as children to explore themselves. For young people, this series will keep their dreams, their wonders, and their awaremenss of the possibilities of life forever strong.

We strongly encourage parents to share the experiences and explorations in the exercises with the young people in their lives. Together, we can all nurture and guide each other into new realms of wonder.

Dragonhawk Publishing

Young Person's School of Magic and Mystery

A Complete Course of Study in Ten Volumes

The Magic of Believing
Dreamtime Magic
Psychic Power
Spirits, Ghosts, and Guardians
Faerie Charms
Star Magic
Healing Arts
Divination and Scrying
Word Magic
Ancient Powers

Ted Andrews

Lesson 1

Do You Believe in Magic?

Have you ever wished upon a star?

Or crossed your fingers?

Have you ever avoided a black cat?

Or knocked on wood?

Wondered if your thoughts made something
    happen?

The truth is everyone believes in magic at some point and those who deny it are usually fibbing or a bit addled.

If you have entered the doors to this school, you probably fit into one or more of the following categories:

➤ You suspect you are magical because you have had some strange things happen around you that you do not understand.

➤ You are curious, wanting to know more about the magical, thinking it may be a way to make your life easier.

➤ You are really skeptical but think it could be fun.

➤ There is a part of you that knows you are special even if others do not recognize it.

Regardless of which of these you may be, if you enter this old mystery school, you'll get a chance to discover things about yourself that will empower you throughout the rest of your life.

The door is open, but it is still up to you to walk through. Understand, though, that there will be work. You will have to invest some time. You will have to practice, but, you will also have fun. And you will surprise yourself with what you can do!

First, let's take some time to define what we are not.

➤ We are NOT a school of wizardry or witchcraft.

➤ We are NOT aligned with any specific tradition or religious dogma.

➤ We are NOT a school of charms and spells.

➤ You will NOT learn incantations here or sorcery of any kind.

➤ There will be NO burning candles to make the boy or girl in your class fall in love with you.

➤ There will be NO trying to turn your little brother or sister into a toad—no matter how much he or she truly deserves it.

➤ There will be NO trying to manipulate friends and family.

In this SCHOOL OF MAGIC AND MYSTERY, you will learn what every magician, shaman, priest, priestess, witch, sorcerer and wise one has had to learn throughout history.

➤ We WILL teach you about the power of your thoughts, imagination and of belief.

➤ We WILL stimulate your mind, and we WILL help you develop your intuition and psychic powers.

➤ We WILL show you how to make and use common magical tools such as words, wands, and staffs for healing, relaxation, and strength.

➤ We WILL reveal the magic of candles and fragrances.

➤ We WILL guide you to use your abilities to make your life more productive and creative.

➤ We WILL help teach you that you are more magical and more wonderful than you ever dreamed.

And if you approach it all with an open heart and mind, you will discover that although life can be hard, it can also enchant. You will find an adventure filled with surprising achievements. The choice will be yours. The magic is already there inside you. What we will teach you is how to let it shine.

Discover
the wonder
and...

believe
once
more!

*Oracle at
Delphi*

About the Entrance Examination

Many people see or hear the word exam and their blood pressure picks up. They get nervous, perspire, and a panicky little voice inside begins to babble:

Remember your last test. You misspelled
your own name...

What if I don't do as well as other people?

What if I cheat and someday I come across one of
the teachers...surely they will know that I
cheated.

What if I'm not really very psychic or magical?

and most importantly:

How can there be a test, when we haven't been
taught anything yet?

Well, the truth is that you have been taught many things. You probably know more about your magical abilities than you realize. As you will discover, there will be much to remember, but there is much to unlearn, and even more to develop. This entrance examination will help you find out whether or not you still believe in magic.

Examination:

Do You Believe in Magic?

Simply answer "Yes" or "No" to the following questions. If you aren't sure about the answer to a question, that's okay. Make note of your uncertainty and move on to the next question.

YES   NO   **?**

YES	NO	?		
☐	☐	☐	1.	Have you ever had an "imaginary" friend?
☐	☐	☐	2.	Have you ever known something would happen before it did?
☐	☐	☐	3.	Do you have "a way with animals"?
☐	☐	☐	4.	Do you believe that animals understand you when you talk with them?
☐	☐	☐	5.	Have you ever been able to tell what others were thinking?
☐	☐	☐	6.	Have you ever felt that trees, flowers, and plants have feelings and sometimes "watch" you?
☐	☐	☐	7.	Have you ever seen lights around people and animals?
☐	☐	☐	8.	Do you associate certain colors with people? (For example, "he's a blue person.")

YES	NO	?	
☐	☐	☐	9. Have you ever dreamt of things before they happened?
☐	☐	☐	10. Do you frequently dream of wild animals and strange beasts, such as dragons?
☐	☐	☐	11. Have you ever felt that you could make things happen if you wished hard enough?
☐	☐	☐	12. Are you confident about playing hunches?
☐	☐	☐	13. Do you frequently get feelings of the "I've been here before" variety?
☐	☐	☐	14. When making choices and decisions, do you logically think them out or do you decide and choose by how you feel at the moment, relying more on your intuition or your own inspiration?
☐	☐	☐	15. Do you ever sense the exact words a person is going to say before they actually say them? Does the sensation later prove itself to be true?
☐	☐	☐	16. Do you believe in telepathy (mind to mind communication), the ability to send and receive thoughts with others?

YES NO **?**

☐ ☐ ☐   17. Have you ever had any clear examples of telepathic communication with another person?

☐ ☐ ☐   18. Have you ever read another person's thoughts correctly?

☐ ☐ ☐   19. Have you ever experienced a feeling that something important was happening at a given moment to someone you knew, although that person was far away?

☐ ☐ ☐   20. When you meet someone for the first time, do you normally get a reaction of either like or dislike for the person? Is this feeling usually accurate?

☐ ☐ ☐   21. Do you believe that specific surroundings such as rooms, houses, or objects can have a special influence on you?

☐ ☐ ☐   22. Are you subject to flashes of insight or perception, which you cannot account for in other ways?

☐ ☐ ☐   23. Have you ever sensed correctly the mood of a friend or family member without any verbal communications?

☐ ☐ ☐   24. Upon meeting someone for the first time, are you able to sense what kind of homelife or childhood this person has had?

YES NO ?

☐   ☐   ☐   25. Have you ever felt you have lived before or have an interest in a particular period of history that you cannot explain?

☐   ☐   ☐   26. Can you tell if something of yours is out of place without actually seeing it or discovering it?

☐   ☐   ☐   27. Have you ever heard voices when no one physically was around and couldn't be explained?

☐   ☐   ☐   28. Are you superstitious and believe that your fate or luck is determined by certain behaviors?

☐   ☐   ☐   29. Have you ever helped someone feel better or been helped to feel better by someone through touch (a hug, a pat on the back, a comforting stroke)?

☐   ☐   ☐   30. Do you think people can heal through touch?

☐   ☐   ☐   31. Do you have or did you ever have a "good luck" charm (object, article of clothing)?

☐   ☐   ☐   32. Do you have a favorite fairy tale or magical story from childhood?

☐   ☐   ☐   33. Are you good at imagining things?

☐   ☐   ☐   34. Are you a daydreamer?

YES	NO	?	
☐	☐	☐	35. Do you believe in angels and other helpful spirit beings?
☐	☐	☐	36. Have you ever been visited by a spirit (someone who has died) while awake or asleep?
☐	☐	☐	37. Is your favorite season of the year autumn or spring?
☐	☐	☐	38. Do you believe in the spirits of Nature (elves, fairies, spirits of trees, and flowers)?
☐	☐	☐	39. Do you believe that the moon and stars affect you?
☐	☐	☐	40. Have you ever wished upon a star (especially a shooting star) and have your wish come true?

Scoring

For every *yes* answer, give yourself 3 points.
For every *no* answer give yourself 1 point.
For every *not sure* answer, give yourself 2 points.

____ YES   X 3 = ____

____ NOT SURE X 2 = ____   ☐ TOTAL

____ NO   X 1 = ____

> The maximum score is 120. If you achieved that, you undoubtedly believe in magic and know that you are already magical, even if you haven't learned to develop it.

> If you score between 90 and 120, you are a person with a strong psychic and magical sense which at one time or another has made its presence felt, even if only vaguely. You will do well to cultivate it.

> If you scored between 60 and 90, you have a stronger than average psychic and magical sense about you. You may suspect you have abilities but may not truly realize it. Your abilities can be developed more clearly if you are willing to apply some effort and learning.

> Any score below 60 indicates that you do not recognize your magical and psychic abilities. There is a tendency to ignore the magic happening around you, and with persistence, a lot of practice, and the right direction, you will be able to bring it out and develop it fully.

The Most Powerful Magic of All

There is a magic more powerful than any other in the world. It is the oldest magic in the world, and everyday it shapes the world and our lives. It creates good fortune, and when not controlled, it brings "bad luck." It heals the sick and helps manifest disease. It can also make us successful or powerless. The most powerful magic of all is the power of our thoughts—the magic of our beliefs.

You say your thoughts are not magical? That they don't have any power? Close your eyes. Go on…close them for a moment. Take a few deep breaths and remember the last time you looked in the mirror and felt you didn't like what you saw.

> Did you feel like staying home and not talking to anyone?

> When you were around other people, did you slouch a little more?

> Or, did you comb your hair down over your face a little more to hide it?

> How did you truly feel?

How do you feel now that just remembering brings back those old feelings.

> Don't you feel a little heavier?

> Are you slouching just a bit more?

That is the power of thought—the power of belief. It affects how we feel and if our thoughts are allowed to grow, they can affect how others respond to us, influencing what happens or doesn't happen for us in life.

Advertisers have known about the power of thoughts and belief for a long time and some adults have used this to their benefit. Take a look at the commercials we see on TV everyday. Advertisers use images and music to manipulate our thoughts and feelings. They try to make us think and feel that our jeans aren't the right brand, our breath isn't fresh enough, our hair isn't full enough or the right color. And let's not even get into the smell of our underarms.

Advertisers "weave a little glamour" (see Lesson 5) to make us feel we aren't good enough without their product. And what do we do? We go out and buy whatever it is—even when we don't need it.

Their magic worked.

But is that magic?

Are our thoughts truly magical?

Do they have power?

Does what we believe really have that great an influence in our lives?

And what actually is magic?

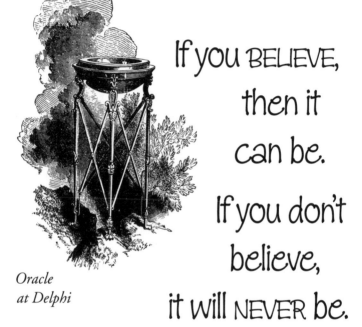

Oracle at Delphi

If you BELIEVE, then it can be. If you don't believe, it will NEVER be.

Remember your favorite fairy tales and the magic that happened in them? The magic in those stories is true...in part. The magic in many of those stories is based on the use of extraordinary power and supernatural forces. This is how many dictionaries define magic, but magic is not supernatural. It does not happen spontaneously. You won't come across a mysterious lamp with a genie that will grant your wishes. Nor are you likely to find a gnome that will spin straw into gold for you.

Magic is the ability to use "nature's wisdom" or "natural energies" to make things happen. It is transformation created through natural laws. Understanding how to make energies and transformations work for us takes a lot of time and practice, but when we combine believing with effort and wisdom, magic does happen!

Just because something isn't seen or understood does not mean it isn't real or won't work. The magic of believing is like the action of magnets. We can put two magnets on a table in front of us and watch the invisible forces associated with them repel and attract each other. These forces are real even though we cannot see them. Magic, like magnetic forces, has its own rules which enable us to direct invisible forces. What we believe and how strongly we believe will attract or repel opportunities, people, and more abundance in our lives.

Magic is natural. How it happens may be hidden from view to most people, but it is real. We just do not completely understand how magic works yet. Think of it like electricity. Most people still do not know how it works, but we do know that it is real. We also know there are electricians who can work with electricity to help us control and direct the lights and heating in our homes to make our lives much more comfortable.

Magicians have learned the wisdom of directing energy to produce specific effects. Like an electrician, they have mastered working with natural forces or energies. True magic is an art, one which actively awakens, strengthens, controls, and directs the energies of life.

The difficulty is in learning to focus and direct the energies. There are many tools and techniques to help us with this. In Lesson 4, we will explore how we can use candles and fragrances to help develop, strengthen, and control our magical abilities until we become skilled enough to do it without these aids.

Of all the tools we can use to help ourselves, none is more important than our own belief. **No magic ever happens without belief.** Magical believing is the practice of using our imagination to create changes in the world around us and to help us direct the energies of life.

Magical believing begins by changing ourselves and our consciousness—by realizing who we truly are and what we truly can do. The art we will teach you in this book is how to believe in your abilities once more and how to use that belief to weave magic more fully into your life.

Magicus Ridiculous

Ridiculous, strange, and amusing
magical practices of the past

How to Acquire
Magical Power

The following Malay invocation must be addressed to the ghost of a murdered man. You first seek out this ghost and then perform a variety of strange rites at the grave. In return, you acquire some magical power from the ghost.

Hearken and assist me;
I am taking this boat to the saints of God,
And I desire to ask for a little magic.

(We can't help but wonder if the ghost were all that magical, couldn't it have prevented itself from being murdered?)

The Rules of Magical Believing

Rules!?

Why are there always rules!?

I can feel your heart sinking as you read this. Yes, there are rules—principles that govern how things work. Part of magic—part of wisdom—is understanding how these rules work. If you don't understand and work with the rules, the magic doesn't create—won't unfold—the way you think it will.

I once met with a lady who used someone's candle spell to bring a new love into her life. She had met a man whom she felt was ideal for her. He was strong and exciting. He seemed to be just what she was looking for.

She did not understand the rules of magic though. Nor did she understand the power of belief. All that she knew was that she wanted a strong, exciting new love in her life. She had been alone long enough. She decided that she had to have this man. What better way of assuring it than through a love spell? It would be quick and easy. She even convinced herself that the love spell would be good for him as well because she would love him more than anyone else.

In less than two months, her love spell worked… kind of. She got a strong man who was very exciting, and at first it was wonderful. In time, though, the relationship became troubled. He was strong, but he was also bullying and somewhat abusive (unbalanced strength). As for the exciting...well...nothing livens up an evening at home more than a few broken dishes and the lights of a police cruiser pulling up to the house. Yes, it was a very exciting relationship.

Had she worked with the rules of magic, had she worked with magical believing rather than using a manipulative spell, she could have avoided a lot of trouble and been more successful at finding love.

The Rules of

1. **If you believe, it can be; if you don't believe, it will never be.**

   Magical energy follows your thoughts. What you think is what you get. What you put out, you get back. The stronger and more often we think and believe something, the stronger and more quickly it will happen—for good or bad.

2. **What we think, do, and believe on one level always affects us on other levels—physically, emotionally, mentally, and spiritually.**

   All things—all parts of our life—are connected. There is a cause and effect relationship to everything. Magic reveals these connections. A shaman who sprinkles a plant with water isn't just "watering the plant." He is also inviting the rains to come. A healer not only works with the body but also the emotional, mental, and spiritual aspects of the person who helped create the problem. Magic helps us to see connections—the causes and effects—and to use them to make our lives more productive.

3. **Our magical beliefs must have a strong foundation.**

   We must be realistic. We must strengthen the possibilities of our beliefs. Through study and practice, we make our beliefs increasingly more probable. If we believe we will win an Oscar but never study acting or do nothing more than local theater performances, we are not laying the foundation for our beliefs to be

Magical Believing

fulfilled. We must put practical effort into our magical activities.

4. **Magic happens in the time, manner, and means that is best for us, if we allow it to.**

   This doesn't mean we do nothing but wait. Our magical beliefs must be acted upon. (See Lesson 3.) We do what we can and then we allow the energy to unfold. Sometimes the effort must be repeated, but each time we act upon our beliefs, successful or not, their power grows. Then, when the time and place is right—most beneficial for us—the energy crystallizes. The magic happens. Most problems with magic occur when people try to force.

5. **You are always more magical than what you believe and more than what others think.**

   As you develop your skills and expand your knowledge, you will find that greater and greater possibilities exist. Once we open the doors to a magical life, it does nothing but grow until it becomes more wonderful than even we imagined.

6. **To have a magical life, you must seek a magical life.**

   Magic is not a hobby, a pastime, or a path to weekend thrills. It is a path of self-discovery. It is a way of life— commitment to a life of enchantment, wonders, and possibilities. It is when we merely dabble in it for fun and thrills that troubles unfold.

The First Tool of Magic

The first and most important tool any person of magic needs is his or her own Book of Enchantment. This is sometimes called *The Magical Journal, The Book of Shadows, Grimoire*, or a variety of other names.

I recommend that you use a Book of Enchantment to record your dreams, wishes, and magical workings. In it you will keep track of the things you do that succeed and those that fail. It is a book that you will be able to draw upon throughout your life, and most good magicians have a number of volumes.

The Book of Enchantment is a tool for confirming your own magical abilities and uniqueness. It will aid you in grounding your mind, body, and spirit after your magical practice. It provides a way to clarify and crystallize your thoughts, desires, hopes, dreams, and wishes so that you can manifest them more fully.

Keeping a Book of Enchantment sends a message to the magical parts of your mind—the subconscious—that you are committed to expressing your magic more fully in your daily life. In this very private book, you can finally acknowledge the magic within you and it eventually becomes a record of your own of magical symbols and images, an ever-growing magical dictionary.

A Book of Enchantment has many other benefits. What you have written can be drawn upon for creative inspiration, helping to bridge the subconscious and conscious minds so our creative magic flows more easily through us. It helps us to crystallize our hope, dreams, and thoughts, and provides a reference so we will know what works and doesn't work in our magical endeavors.

As we record our thoughts in our Book of Enchantment, we improve our ability to communicate with the deeper levels of the mind and with people outside of us. Through it, we can link our deep and magical inner mind to our outer world activities. We can also use our Book of Enchantment to interpret, create, and use magical symbols and images to affect our lives more dynamically.

Magical and symbolic images are some of the more common tools that all magicians learn to use. Symbolic images or actions are those that mean more than what they appear to on the surface. For example, some shamans ritually pour water onto dry earth or over a plant that is drying up while saying special prayers. Although it may seem that the prayers and activity are to save the plant, it is much more. It is a magical act, symbolizing the bringing of rains to the environment.

All images and symbols contain magical seeds. They are links to energies throughout the universe. When we give an image or symbol special significance, its magic is awakened. We give it this special significance through regular use in meditation, ritual, prayer, action, or artwork. The greater the significance we attach to an image or symbol, the greater the power it will have in our lives. Its magic grows.

Think of yourself as being split in two. You have an outer self, the self most people are aware of. You also have an inner, magical self. This is a part of you that most people never seem to recognize. (And sometimes we don't even recognize that part of ourselves.) To make our lives magical, we must create a bridge so that the two parts of us can come together.

Symbols and images are the magical language of the mind, and it is the only language the magical part of us truly understands. Magical symbols and images bridge the inner and the outer parts of ourselves. They also connect us to energies outside of us. Our work with the magical symbols and images serves as a magnet, drawing those outside energies into our life.

Confusing?

Think of it this way. By using the magical symbols and images, you first join your outer self with your inner magical self. When they are joined, they become a magnet drawing into your life the energies associated with the symbol—the energies of the universe.

Remember the second rule of magic from the table? Everything we think, do, and believe affects us on other levels. When we focus on an image or symbol, it links us to all of the energies associated with it, not just the part we are focused upon.

We will learn more about magical images in Lesson 2 when you will create your own castle. It will be a place where you can awaken the magical part of yourself more easily. Although it will be your own unique sacred place, it will bridge you to the energies and aspects of all sacred places everywhere throughout time.

*Oracle
at Delphi*

It is not enough to believe in God.

You must also know that God believes in you!

Magical Practice

The Book of Enchantment

SKILLS
DEVELOPED

- **strengthens beliefs**
- **helps in creating your own magical formulas**
- **provides a reference for what works for you and what does not**
- **increases creativity**
- **improves communication**

There are many ways of setting up your Book of Enchantment. The following are guidelines only. I do recommend that the Book of Enchantment be handwritten, but I am a bit old school. I know many people that keep their Book of Enchantment in their computer. One is neither better nor worse than any other. Do whatever is easiest for you.

Begin by obtaining a book of blank pages. Most gift shops or bookstores sell these. You may wish to decorate the book in a style that is your own. You will probably find that as you work on it, additions will be made over the months and hopefully years in which you keep your Book of Enchantment, eventually collecting many volumes.

CREATING YOUR
BOOK OF ENCHANTMENT

1. **In the front, write a dedication.**

   Dedicate it to helping you to understand and express your own magic and wonder in your life. Some people include a spiritual verse or a favorite bit of writing.

   The following magical effects are likely to occur just from performing steps 2, 3, and 4 in this Book of Enchantment setup:

   ✓ Within several days you will have dreams of things and people you had forgotten about.

   ✓ You may also have repeats of dreams from your childhood.

   ✓ Over the following week, you will remember more and more things to add to each list, seeming to come out of the blue—while you are in the midst of other activities.

   ✓ Friends from your past will contact you or be encountered.

2. **After the dedication, leave several blank pages and on the top of the next blank page, write the title of this first section, WHAT I USED TO BELIEVE IN.**

   Underneath the heading, begin listing everything you used to believe in no matter how silly. Pick a time (about a half hour) when you will be alone to do this.

Magical Practice

You will be surprised how many things you believed in. If you are not sure if you believed in them, or just wanted to but never did, list them also. Try to add to this list periodically. If you can, make a note next to all those you can about why you quit believing in them. What happened and when?

3. **Leave another four to five pages blank, and on the top of the next blank page, write the title of this second section, WHAT I NOW BELIEVE IN.**

    Make a list of these things. If you are like most people, it will be a much smaller list than the first one. It is often like this at first. In time, you will find this list grows larger than the first. When you awaken your magical believing, so much more becomes possible in life. (Leave about four to five pages blank to add to this section in the months to come.)

4. **Leave another four to five pages blank, and on the top of the next blank page, write the title of this third section, MY HOPES, WISHES, AND DREAMS.**

    In this section, make a list of all the things you hoped, wished, or dreamed to do in your life. Don't worry about how silly or ridiculous they may seem. List them all. As you will discover in time, we are never given a hope, wish, or dream without also being given an opportunity to make it a reality.

The Book of Enchantment (cont.)

5. **Throughout the remaining pages of the book, keep a record of your magical activities.**

    If you do nothing more than the magical practices in this book, you will have plenty to write about. Keep track of the day and date you perform each magical practice. Over the following few days, pay attention to how people treat you.

    As your magical energy is awakened, it affects your aura (the energy surrounding your body), making it more vibrant. People will respond to you more strongly. You may find yourself more noticed in all you do. You will find others commenting more and responding more to you.*

6. **Every couple of days, after performing one of the magical practices, look over the events of your life since then.**

    Examine how you are feeling and how others are responding. Make note of everything in your Book of

---

* Sometimes in life we encounter people who do not like us. We all wish this wasn't so, but it happens. When we start awakening our magical selves, these people sometimes respond even more strongly and negatively. At some level they recognize a power awakening within us. Even though they do not understand it or even realize it, it triggers a response in them. It is threatening to them and they respond accordingly.

    If this happens, remain calm. Ignore it as best as possible. Avoid the person and just continue your magical work. In time, your energy will be such that the person's own negativity will come back upon them. They will become their own worst enemy.

Ted Andrews   31

The Book of Enchantment (cont.)

Enchantment, no matter how silly it may seem. In time, your changing energy will become more obvious. People will respond more strongly and positively to you. You will find less stress, and you will find yourself accomplishing more.

No one has to read your BOOK OF ENCHANTMENT. It is private and it is yours. It is your personal record of your own magical awakening. It can be in any style you want. Feel free to decorate it and write in it at times other than after the magical practices.

Be careful about sharing your magical practices. Not everyone is receptive. Avoid going to school and telling everyone your are learning to "perform magic." This is a sure way of blocking further growth and success through the negative thoughts of others and through your own bragging.

If others ask, tell them simply what you are doing. If your parents wonder, show them a copy of this book. Talk to them about it, and remember that nothing in this book is negative or "evil." It is all about bringing out your greatest potentials.

SUGGESTIONS FOR PARENTS

➤ Create a BOOK OF ENCHANTMENT for yourself. Young people learn by the examples we set. When children and teens see parents reading regularly, they become more interested in reading. The same is true for journalling and other activities.

➤ Share what you write in the sections

WHAT I USED TO BELIEVE IN,

WHAT I NOW BELIEVE IN, and

MY HOPES, WISHES, AND DREAMS with each other.

Go first. Make it a special day. It will encourage your sons or daughters to share and it will make them more comfortable in the sharing. You will be surprised what you learn about each other.

➤ Set a regular time in which you will work on the exercises with the young person in your life. Keep it light and fun. After the exercises and meditations, share, and compare.

Lesson 2

The
Magic Wand

Wouldn't it be great to have a magic wand?

We could just wave it around and our problems
would disappear. If we needed something, we
could shake it about and it would appear out of
nowhere.

If such a thing were possible, I would have turned my
brothers into worms on more than one
occasion while growing up.

Magic wands have come in many sizes, shapes, and models throughout the ages. Some mystics and shamans used a simple staff. Some Wiccans use the branch of a willow tree. Magicians of the past have used swords or even a finger of their hand. Sorcerers and medicine people have used feathers and bones. Modern psychics make and use quartz crystal wands.

Our Mind Is Our Greatest Magic Wand

What we often do not realize is that the wand or magical staff is just a tool and not the source of the magical energy. The wand simply helps to focus and direct magical energy and even that is not really needed. Our own mind is our greatest magic wand since, as we learned in Lesson 1, our mind weaves into action so much of what comes into our lives.

The ancient Hebrews gave different names for how God manifested in the world. One of these names is *Jehovah Aloah Va Daath*, which is freely translated as "God made manifest in the sphere of the mind." The mind is at the heart of our lives, at the heart of our health and well being, and at the heart of our successes and failures. What we think and believe sets the energy in motion for what we will experience in life. We can learn to use our mind like a magic wand to help make things happen.

Inside each of us is a subconscious which monitors processes of the mind we are normally unaware of, such as a subconscious wish. Our subconscious mind controls over 90 percent of what manifests in our bodies and our life circumstances. We tell ourselves, "I get two colds every winter." The subconscious mind immediately begins working with your body so as winter approaches you are more likely to "catch" those two colds.

The subconscious mind responds literally to what we think, feel, say, and believe. You tell your friends you "lost ten pounds" and that inner part of you, your subconscious, perks up its ears:

"Lost? Lost? I better go find them!"

It then proceeds to find those ten pounds you lost, and it usually throws in a few extra pounds just in case you lose them again.

Believing
is seeing!

Like
attracts like!

Your Mind is
Your Magic
Wand

All energy
follows
thought!

What you put out,
you get back!

Change your imaginings
and you change
your world!

ᛘ**Magicus Ridiculous**

Ridiculous, strange, and amusing
magical practices of the past

Magical Wands

For magical flight take the oak rod [the magician's magic wand], turn in the direction in which you want to fly, and write the name of your destination on the ground.

Key of Solomon (medieval grimoire)

As a charm against an eagle's attack, the sorcerer Lemminkainen took the feathers of a black fowl and he leisurely rubbed the feathers and he created a flock of grouse.

Kalevala (Finnish epic)

To charm a child against mischief, a superstitious woman will lift the baby from the cradle. Then by the action of her middle finger upon the child's forehead and through her purifying spittle on the lips of the child (slobbering upon them), she "skillfully" checks the evil eye.

Persius (34-62 C.E.)

The Power of Creative Imagination

Creative imagination is the ability to use our minds to make images of what we want in life. It is the ability to picture, imagine, or just think about something in a way that brings it to mind clearly on some level. Through creative imagination, we learn to use our mind like a magic wand. In magical practices, the creative imagination has many forms and many names, including thought projection, pathworking, and even magical daydreaming.

Creative imagination is the key to opening the doors to the magical and spiritual realms, the ability to tap into a reality in some form and on some level beyond the normal world we usually perceive. With creative imagination, we bring about a new awareness, a new kind of experience in form and color. We awaken our higher possibilities. There are five primary keys to working with our creative imagination:

➤ practice
➤ relaxation
➤ visualizations
➤ concentration, and
➤ grounding.

PRACTICE

We must practice our creative imaginings. It takes a little time everyday. You do not have to visualize and imagine several hours in order to get results. Five to ten minutes per day is all that it takes.

The first thing in the morning and the last thing at night are wonderful times to practice it. In the morning before climbing out of bed, take a few minutes to perform your imagining and visualization. It sets the tone and energy for the day. At night as you go to sleep, perform your creative imagining again.

Try not to work on too many things at once. Choose one simple thing first to visualize and imagine about and work on it. Because this kind of visualization can be done in five to ten minutes, it does not have to interfere with the other exercises you may do.

Even though it may not seem like you have enough time in the day to do everything, don't worry. You are working on creating a magical lifetime. You will have plenty of time to work on all aspects of it at some point. Experiment with each of the exercises, and then choose one or two to focus on.

RELAXATION

Relaxation is crucial for any magic to work. Stress and worry block the flow of energy. The more relaxed we are, the easier it is to concentrate and project and so when we are relaxed, energy manifests better.

Progressive relaxation and rhythmic breathing are an essential part of our training in creating a magical life. With practice, your body will respond automatically. You will be using the progressive relaxation and rhyth mic breathing in the magical practices (exercises) in this book.

Also keep in mind that without relaxation, we cannot tap into the subconscious mind of our magical inner self. Only through relaxation (through practiced shifting of our focus from the outer to the inner) can we bring the magic out.

Visualizations

For magic to become truly powerful in our life, we must visualize as clearly as possible—making our thoughts and images as lifelike as possible.

For example, close your eyes. Now think about an orange. Try to visualize its shape, its size, and color. In your mind, think about how the peel feels. Notice the rough, pimpled texture as you press your fingers into the orange to peel it. Bring to mind the fragrance. Can you smell it? Now bring to mind its taste in your mouth

If you are using your mind to create prosperity, you must visualize—imagine—yourself as if you are already wealthy. Imagine, see, and feel yourself this way. Visualize all of the things you will be doing with your prosperity.

If you are using your mind to heal yourself, you must visualize yourself as strong and healthy. See, imagine, and feel yourself doing the things you cannot do now. Visualize all of the things you can do by being healthy.

CONCENTRATION

We should be able to focus on the image without other thoughts intruding. Now, since we are all human, this is not always possible. Distractions can always pop up that break our concentration. It may be a brother or sister banging on your door. It could be thoughts of the test you took that day or any number of things.

If you find yourself distracted, just take a deep breath and bring your focus back to your visualization. In time, you will find your concentration stronger and you will find that other people and outside situations are much less distracting.

Be aware that when you are working with the meditations and magical practice, you are learning to control the subconscious mind. At some point, you will encounter resistance. For most people, the subconscious mind follows whatever whim it has. When you use meditation, magical practices, rituals, and other techniques for directing the subconscious, it will resist. We may experience an itch, worry over homework or friends will pop up, thoughts of not having enough time, and doubts about the reality and effectiveness of what we're doing are but a few of the distractions. The mind will try and wander.

When you become distracted, do not get upset. Simply persist, bringing your focus back to the images and scenarios you are working on. Eventually the resistance will diminish. The subconscious mind is often like a little child trying to get its own way. But we can train the subconscious mind through consistent and calm correction of its wanderings.

We only encounter resistance when we have tapped into the subconscious mind. Recognize the resistance, the mind wanderings, as a sign that you have accessed your inner magical self. Then bring your attention back to your point of focus and continue with the exercise. You are training the magical part of you to work along the lines you decide. Persistence is the key.

GROUNDING

All of our magical efforts need to be grounded. So much of our work begins in the inner mind, but it also must be anchored in the outer world. This is called grounding, which helps to prevent that "spacey" kind of feeling following meditations. Grounding also releases more solidly the magical energy we have been working with into our physical life.

Remember we are physical beings, and everything manifests to us through the physical at some point. Work with the magical and spiritual should never imply neglect of the physical.

You will be using the grounding rituals also in your magical practices. See pages 42 to 43 for a more detailed explanation of these rituals. The grounding should also have a simple positive statement. Affirmations are posi tive statements that something is already so. For example, look at the following statements.

I will get a wonderful, new job.

I will be healthier and magical by next year.

I am prosperous, magical, and healthy.

Which are truly effective affirmations? Of these three statements, only the third is a true affirmation. It simply states you are a particular way—right now. The other two refer to the future, which never gets here. It will always be in the future and will never happen. We live in the present. When you make your statement, visualize or imagine yourself as already being that way. Believe it. Feel it. Get truly emotional about it.

 I am magical!

Remember that your mind is a magic wand. How you use it or don't use it affects what you accomplish or don't accomplish. Your mind affects everything that happens to you. Yes, there are some things that cannot be controlled. We cannot affect the free-will choices of others, but magic helps us to live well with what we have available and opens doors to possibilities.

*Oracle at
Delphi*

We are never given
a hope, wish or
dream,
without also
being given
opportunities
to make them
a reality.

Beginning and Ending Your

Set the Mood

(preparing for the exercise)

Begin a magical practice by finding a time to be by yourself when you will not be disturbed or interrupted. You may wish to set the tone by using candles or fragrances.

Relaxation

(beginning the exercise)

There are two kinds of relaxation techniques used to begin the exercises. Use the method that works best for you.

progressive relaxation

Make yourself comfortable. Take a few slow, deep breaths and send warm, soothing thoughts to every part of your body, starting with your feet and moving to the top of your head. Visualize warm, soothing energy melting up over you from your feet to your head. Take your time with this. The more relaxed you are the more quickly and easily you will succeed.

rhythmic breathing

Inhale slowly through the nostrils, hold the breath, and then exhale slowly through the mouth. Imagine warm, soothing energy flowing to every part of your body. As you relax, allow your attention to be focused entirely upon yourself.

Magical Practices (EXERCISES)

GROUNDING RITUAL
(ENDING THE EXERCISE)

Altered states tend to draw us away from the physical, so after our magical practices, we need to ground, to reconnect with the physical world.

Grounding should always involved a little stretching. Eating a few crackers is also helpful. By eating something light, the body begins to focus on digestion, which also helps ground us.

Writing in your Book of Enchantment about your feelings and observations after an exercise also grounds those energies into the physical.

The grounding should also involve some vocal expression of affirmation and gratitude. This can be a prayer of thanks for what already is.

Castle's Keep

SKILLS
DEVELOPED

- stimulates the imagination
- awakens creativity
- creates a place of peace when life is stressful
- provides a sacred place in heart and mind to explore all of your magical potential

Every magician has a sacred place where powers and magic can be awakened, harnessed, and directed. This sacred place always begins in the mind. It will then extend to a special prayer room or altar space where magical exercises, meditations, and prayers can be performed.

Our sacred place can also lead us to other realms and dimensions (including time). In our sacred place, we are safe and can work to understand the things in life which confuse us. In this safe environment, we can develop our intuition and strengthen the knowledge of our own magical abilities.

This sacred place always begins in the mind through the use of *creative imagination.* Creative imagination is the ability of the mind to create images and scenes associated with an idea, thought, or purpose. It is essential to awakening our magical potential. It is what helps us connect to spiritual energies and beings of the universe.

The key, though, is to make the images and scenes three-dimensional and as real in the mind as possible. Think of it like a concentrated daydream or a very clear and memorable night dream. In time, these images become stronger and more powerful, affecting us physically, emotionally, mentally, and spiritually.

In this exercise, we will create a castle as our sacred place. As you work with your Castle's Keep, your sacred place may take on its own characteristics and qualities. And it should, but we need to start somewhere. I like the castle because I have worked with it for most of my life and it lends itself to so many aspects of magical and spiritual development. It becomes a wonderful place of possibilities.

From this place, we will learn to take journeys and create wondrous stories. The amazing thing is that these journeys and stories will release magical energy into our lives if we work with them in special ways.

We will begin by outlining some of the features of your castle. You may wish to have a section in your Book of Enchantment for this. You may even wish to have a separate book. When I first did this as a kid, I called it "Castle's Keep," and I had almost an entire journal describing the castle and its various functions. Over the years, I would add to it and change it.

You may find it helpful to make drawings of your castle and the various places within it. You may wish to find photos of similar castles or castles you have imagined. In time you will want to have a name for your castle, as all castles have names, but keep it a secret. This gives your safe haven more power and makes it more special.

Every part of your castle will have a function. It will be a place where you can go to awaken greater abilities and to understand more about yourself and the world around you. It will take time to become familiar with your castle and all of its chambers and magical secrets. So be patient and have fun with it.

LOCATION OF THE CASTLE

Decide where you want your castle located. It should be a place not easily accessible so it can be well-guarded and protected. It should be a place which allows you to see if outsiders are approaching. Remember, this is your safe and sacred place, a place where no one can enter without your permission.

My castle is located on a great cliff overlooking the sea on one side and a great fertile valley on the other. I have secret paths down the cliffs to the shore where I can sail to different times and places—for such things as past life exploration, dream travel, and astral projection. It also gives me access to the waters for communing with the merfolk, the great dragons, and other sea creatures.

Castle's Keep (cont.)

BEYOND THE CASTLE

The grounds beyond the castle should be expansive, seeming to be never ending, symbolizing all of the possibilities available. In my castle haven, I created a fertile valley on the opposite side of the cliff and beyond that a great forest.

In the fertile valley, I have an orchard and gardens where I can go to stimulate new growth in different areas of my life. If I need some abundance in my life, I go to the orchard and harvest some of the fruit. This in turn triggers opportunities for increase and abundance in the following week within my outer life.

The forest is where I go to commune and learn about Nature or to work with animals, herbs, and even the Faerie Realm. Over the years, this forest has taken on many new dimensions and a life of its own. I discover lakes and waterfalls and surprising beings that I did not imagine or create. It is also one of the places I go when I have to confront fears.

THE CASTLE ITSELF

As with all castles, yours should have many rooms, halls, and chambers. Each is a magical place, a place where you can do special things. The following rooms are suggestions for some of the possible inner chambers and how they might be used.

Magical Practice

Library

Every castle should have a great library. Here books and knowledge from around the world can be studied and absorbed. This is my favorite place within the castle. My library is a great circular hall with row after row of ancient and modern books, scrolls, and other writings. I also have my books speak to me. As I run my hands over the various volumes, they whisper to me, enticing me to read them. Through this room we can open to the *Akashic Records*, the place where everything from every life in the universe is recorded.

Great Hall

In the great hall you may sit and speak with teachers and others whom you invite. It can be a great place to visit with spirit guides, inviting them in so that you may learn more about them. I also visit the Great Hall when I need to take several things into careful consideration or to set energy in motion in my daily life to help me make important decisions.

Turrets

Turrets are special rooms for whatever you wish them to be. One of my turrets is the "Turret of the Star" where I go to learn about the stars and to discover astrological influences affecting my life.

Castle's Keep (cont.)

Bed Chamber

This is a place to relax, heal, and explore dreams. The bed chamber is also a place for romance. When I do dreamwork, particularly to dream answers to problems, I will use this room.

Courtyard

Castle courtyards have many functions and can be a place to invite merriment and social activities into our life. They can be used for outdoor ceremonies and rituals.

Gardens

Every castle has special gardens and each serves its own purpose, from simple pleasure to healing. I have a Faerie Garden, a Garden of Prayer, a Garden of Play, just to name a few.

Chapel or Sacred Circle

Every castle should have a place for prayer, ritual, and ceremony. This can be indoors or outdoors. It can be associated with a particular tradition: Christian, Jewish, Muslim, Wiccan, and so on. Your castle can have places for various traditions. Mine has a temple for working with the Qabala as well as a more traditional chapel more in line with the Catholic tradition in which I was raised.

Magical Practice

My chapel has an outdoor altar, a circle for Wiccan-style ceremonies, and a medicine wheel for Native American ceremonies. Yours should be a place of prayer that is comfortable for you and is suitable to your own beliefs.

There are other things to be found within the castle. You may have an armory for building shields and protection for you and those you love. You may have a moat to discourage uninvited visitors and to help control who or what you allow into your sacred castle.*

As you develop this castle, this sacred place, it will become an energy that surrounds everything you do. It is not a place for escaping daily life, but for working with your daily life more effectively and creatively.

It takes time to create this castle and to learn all of its secrets. I am still learning about hidden parts of my castle and I have been working with it most of my life. It always surprises me. But it is a place in which I still find great peace, understanding, and magical wonders.

---

* As an author, I often have people trying to "tune into me" or project things in my direction. My castle is set up for protection and privacy so no one gets in without specific invitation. This protection has been built into my castle on many levels over many, many years.

Castle's Keep (cont.)

BRINGING YOUR CASTLE TO LIFE

- *Set the mood.*
- *Perform a progressive relaxation.*

1. **Create a link from where you are meditating to the castle.**

   There are many ways of doing this. One is by visualizing a door forming opposite you. It opens, inviting you to enter. Visualize yourself—imagine yourself—stepping through that doorway. As you do, you find yourself standing at the castle's gate.

   I often use a doorway that leads from where I am meditating through a secret passageway, up a spiral staircase to the attic. It doesn't have to be that complicated, I just like the idea of secret passages. I think they're fun! Another link to your castle might be a drawbridge that lowers to allow you to enter.

2. **Spend some time—about ten to fifteen minutes—exploring the castle.**

   The time will pass quickly. Don't be in a hurry. You have an entire lifetime to learn the ins and outs of this wonderful place. Make the castle as amazing and as colorful as you want.

3. **When you are ready to leave, find any closed door and stand before it.**

   Visualize the room where you began this meditation on the other side of the door. Open the door and step back through. Feel yourself back in your room. Take several slow deep breaths and begin to stretch and move slowly.

* *Perform a grounding ritual.*

   Write in your Book of Enchantment about your visit. Record anything you felt or experienced during this first visit to the castle.

From this castle—from this sacred space—we will take many journeys. These journeys will have the ability to release energies into our lives. The images and symbols in these journeys are like light switches. When we use them, we flip on the switch and the energy flows.

 Throughout this book, we will learn some specific ways of using this castle for such things as time travel and awakening your psychic powers. But there are

Castle's Keep (cont.)

many other uses which will unfold as you grow and develop your magic.

For now, though, repeat this exercise, exploring more of the castle, at least three times in the following week. Then continue exploring once or twice a week for the rest of the month.

Just exploring the castle this one time will have several wonderful benefits. Most importantly, it sends a wake-up message to the magical part of you that has probably been sleeping for some time. It says that you are serious about creating a magical life.

You start the process of bringing the magical part of you to life more fully with each visit. You will awaken your creativity and you will have a sense of "coming home." In the following days and weeks of using this exercise, you will begin to feel calmer, more self-assured, and more in control of your life.

Fire and Ice

SKILLS
DEVELOPED

- **strengthens mind power**
- **stimulates creative imagination**
- **improves the ability to control and direct energy**
- **increases control of body responses**

Do you believe it's possible to change your temperature in a few minutes time simply by the power of your thoughts and imagination?

Do you believe it's possible to change the temperature in the air around you just through the power of your imagination?

If you could do either of these, do you think you might begin to believe in even more possibilities?

Most people have forgotten or don't realize how strong the mind is and how much it can do for us. We have forgotten how to believe in its possibilities. We often don't know how to believe in our own power. Believing must be practiced. It's the only way to strengthen our true magic wand (our creative imagination).

This exercise will help you learn to believe in your power once more as it reveals possibilities rarely even imagined. Through regular practice, you will develop the ability to change your body's temperature with increasing speed and ease. You will even learn to affect the temperature of the air around you. You will also develop greater control over how the world and other people affect you. On more advanced levels, you are learning to control the elements of fire and air.

You may wish to set the mood for this exercise by using an appropriate candle or incense, as described in Lesson 4. Either white or blue candles are good choices. Both are colors for heat and cold (white hot and white with cold, or blue flame and blue with cold).

For this exercise you will need a thermometer that can be easily held within your hands so your skin actually touches the glass part. Ideally, it should also be easy to read. You will be learning to raise and lower temperature with the power of your mind through your creative imagination. I've also included two variations for this exercise, one that you can do with a partner.

You will not need a great deal of time for this exercise. It is best to perform the exercise for ten to fifteen minutes at a time, once or twice a day. This exercise also works best if you have fun while performing it. Do not take it seriously. (I have never had anyone not be able to do this after two or three tries.)

Magical Practice

CHANGING YOUR
BODY TEMPERATURE

• *Set the mood.*

• *Perform a slow,
progressive relaxation.*

1. **Look at the thermometer and make a mental note of
the temperature.**

   Then set it on your lap or somewhere you can easily
   take hold of it while in the midst of the following
   meditation.

2. **Breathe deeply, close your eyes, and let the following
   scene unfold in your mind.**

   Some people like to read the meditation through
   several times to get it firmly in their mind before
   visualizing it. Some like to record it and perform it
   while listening to the recording. Experiment. Find
   what works best for you.

Fire and Ice (cont.)

As you begin to relax, in your mind's eye you see a door in front of you. You stand up and step through the door. You find yourself standing in the garden courtyard of your castle. There is a sense of freedom, of coming home. You look about at the castle surrounding you and are filled with wonder at the growing sense of all things being possible here.

You take a seat on a nearby bench, enjoying the beauty of the courtyard. You are surprised to see your thermometer sitting on the bench, but then in your castle anything is possible. You pick it up and hold it between your hands.

(At this point pick up your thermometer and hold it between your hands.)

The sun is high overhead and you feel its warmth upon you, soft and soothing. The sun warms your head and chest, and you can actually feel the individual rays of sunshine touching and spreading throughout your body, radiating from your chest outward in all directions. The warmth spreads down to your feet and up to the top of your head, energizing and soothing you at the same time. You feel the warm energy of the sun touching and filling every cell within your body.

You breathe deeply the warm air and feel the sun's energy and heat beginning to grow a little stronger. You close your eyes in the courtyard and raise your face to the sun. You feel the warmth growing, and you feel the air around you. No longer is it just empty space, but substance that is growing warmer as well.

With each breath, the air grows warmer about you. The energy of the sun upon you grows stronger. It is not uncomfortable. In fact, it is energizing.

Ted Andrews

Magical Practice

You can feel your body absorbing the heat, adjusting to it, and radiating it out, as if you are becoming a living sun yourself. You feel your body absorbing the heat and the warmth spreading throughout your body.

You feel as if your hands can direct this heat in any way you desire. You feel the heat in your hands growing stronger. If you were holding a candy bar, the chocolate would melt and drip over your fingers. An ice cube would turn to water. And still the heat grows.

As you look around the courtyard you see the ground shimmering like the heat off the highway on a hot summer's day. As you breathe deeply, exhaling, steam comes out of your mouth in soft swirls. You blow a little harder and you see a tiny flame. For a moment you see yourself as a fire-breathing dragon. And you laugh, and when you do, the heat pours out of you.

As you hold the thermometer, with the heat pouring through your hands, you see the temperature rising. One degree. Two degrees. Five degrees. Ten. Your fingers move while holding the thermometer and you see small sparks of heat. Your hands are so warm...so hot...you are sure that by touching something you could set it on fire.

Your mind is filled with images of heat and fire...summer's day...a campfire...a forest fire...the desert...a volcano...a thousand suns...all of them are alive within you!

See it. Feel it. Imagine it and know that it is real. You feel the heat inside you growing, but it is not uncomfortable. It is healing and strengthening. You feel the heat flowing through your hands.

Fire and Ice (cont.)

You see it like flames of light and the temperature of the thermometer rises more.

**(Now look at the thermometer and make a mental
note of the temperature reading.)**

*You breathe deeply, mentally pulling back some of that heat. A
cloud passes over the sun, and there is a brush of cool air. The heat
begins to diminish. More clouds move in, blocking the sunlight
and you cannot tell whether the sun is setting or the clouds are just
blocking it entirely.*

*You lift your face to the sky, watching the clouds thicken. You
breathe deeply, enjoying the coolness of the breeze that comes with
the clouds. As you breathe in the cool air, you exhale the warmth.
You feel the coolness growing.*

*The air is crisp and sweet. Your breath cools. You feel yourself
growing alert, as if awakening from a deep sleep. The growing
coolness is calming, and you feel your blood cooling.*

*The wind grows a little stronger, with a cool bite to it. You
breathe deeply, taking more of the coolness into you. It is not
uncomfortable, and you enjoy how it flows through your body.*

*As you look about you in the courtyard, you see a soft frost on
the ground. You can see your breath, and there is a tingling in
your fingertips and toes, feelings you have had at times when you
have been outside too long in the cold. But you know this feeling is
not harmful to you while you are in this castle.*

*You feel the cold moving in and out of
you with each breath. You reach out
and touch a flower and icy crystals form
a beautiful and exotic patterns upon it.
You are calm and cool, and there is a*

Ted Andrews

Magical Practice

sense that nothing could ever upset you. You see the world and people in your life coolly.

See it. Feel it. Imagine it and know that it is real.

As you breathe out, your breath crystallizes and drops to the ground in glistening snow. You feel your blood now—not as warm red—but ice blue. You feel the coolness pouring through your hands and you feel the thermometer icing up.

You look at the temperature, and it has begun to drop. Two degrees. Five degrees. Ten.

(Now look at the thermometer again to note the change in temperature.)

Your mind is filled with images of cold and ice. Ice cubes. Frost. Snowfalls. Blizzards. The Arctic. The cold is alive within you and around you.

You are filled with wonder. Is it all that easy? And a part of you knows that it really is…and this is just the beginning. And as you realize this, the clouds begin to shift. The sun begins to peak through. The cold begins to shift.

You feel your body returning to normal. Your breath is neither hot nor cold. You are balanced. The air around you is comfortable and calm. The courtyard has returned to normal and you look at the thermometer and are amazed that the temperature has returned to where it was when you began.

(Check the temperature and make a note of it at this point.)

You smile and stand up. This truly is a magical place! And for the first time in a long time you feel stronger and more capable. A growing sense of hope

Fire and Ice (cont.)

and possibility is filling you and there is no doubt that in the days ahead, this castle and your life will only grow more powerful and more magical.

You breathe deeply and walk across the courtyard and stand before a door. You can see yourself sitting, meditating on the other side. You smile because you know that each time you return from the castle you will grow ever more magical in your daily life.

You open the door and step through.

Breathe deeply, feeling yourself back within your room.

You feel strong, balanced, and strengthened. You slowly begin to stretch and move. There is within you a sense that in time you will be able to project heat and cold through your hands and body to any degree you imagine. And you are filled with wonder!

- *Perform a grounding ritual.*

    Do not worry if your scenario is a little bit different or if you did not remember everything in it. Each time you do this, it will get easier. Take some time now and record what you felt and what happened to the temperature in your Book of Enchantment.

    Some people keep a record of the temperature changes so they can see their progress over the coming weeks.

Magical Practice

VARIATION WITH COLOR BREATHING

A variation of this exercise can be performed through color breathing and candles. Place a red candle and a white candle in front of you. Light the red candle. Note the temperature of the thermometer, then cup it between your hands.

1. **Focus on the red candle and begin a slow, rhythmic breathing.**

   Inhale slowly through the nostrils, hold and then exhale slowly through the mouth. As you inhale, see and feel yourself breathing in warm red light and energy. Imagine it filling and warming your body. As you exhale, visualize that warm energy pouring through your hands and warming the thermometer, raising the temperature. (Focus only on the candle.)

   Repeat this for four to five minutes and then check the temperature of the thermometer.

2. **Extinguish the red candle and allow the thermometer to return to normal.**

3. **Light the white candle and perform the same breathing technique as with the red, only allowing cool white, frosty energy to fill you as you breathe in, and send it out through the hands as you exhale.**

Fire and Ice (cont.)

VARIATION FOR PARTNERS

Another variation of this exercise can help partners to work on changing the other person's temperature for them. This exercise can also be used to begin to develop healing touch, or the ability to send mental messages (telepathy).

One of you sits, holding the thermometer. The other sits behind with hands either on the head or with palms pressed against the back of the one holding the thermometer.

1. **The partner with hands on the head or back begins rhythmic breathing.**

    Breathe in for a count of four, hold for a count of four, and exhale for a count of four. As you exhale, send warm energy through your hands into the body of your partner.

2. **After three to five minutes, check the change in the thermometer.**

3. **Repeat the process, sending cold energy.**

4. **Then switch positions and repeat the exercise.**

SUGGESTIONS FOR PARENTS

➤ Create a sacred place, an altar, or meditation area, in your home. (It is O.K. if your young person wants a scared place in his or her room.) Go together to purchase candles and other accessories. Visit a New Age or metaphysical store to find books and items for the magical library in your castle.

➤ Take a candle-making class together so that you can make candles for your sacred place and for the various exercises.

➤ Practice the "Fire and Ice" exercise together as partners, working to change the other person's temperature for them. See the section on "A Special Variation for Partners" section in that exercise for more details.

➤ Practice affirming the magic in each other and your lives by telling each other fun, magical things everyday. Have fun with it. Be silly, be spontaneous and be imaginative.

Affirmation
Fun

There are fairies dancing
about your head.

The ghost took my homework and
so I couldn't finish it.

You aura is shining brightly.

Lesson 3

Making Wishes Come True

Star Light, Star Bright,
    First star I see tonight.
Wish I may, wish I might,
    Grant this wish I wish tonight.

Make a wish and blow out the candles.

See a shooting star and make a wish.

If a ladybug lights on you, make a wish. When it flies
    away, the wish will come true.

Find and keep the first violet of spring and the fairies
    will work to make your wishes come true
    throughout the year.

Upon your first look at a new moon, make a wish,
    and within a year it will be fulfilled.

People make wishes for many things. Sometimes it
seems as if we make up reasons just to make wishes. It is
fun, but how many people actually believe their wishes
will come true?

Belief is necessary if wishes are to come true. The
power of believing bridges our magical self to our outer

The Monkey's Paw

One of my favorite tales is a spooky story about a man given the paw of a monkey and told it will grant three wishes. He is also warned to be careful.

When he gets home to his family, he tells them about it, and they encourage him to wish for money. Before he goes to bed that night, he holds the monkey's paw in his hand and wishes for lots of money.

Several days later a lawyer appears at his home. He brings both good and bad news. First, he informs the man that his mother had died several nights before. (Yes, on the night he made his wish). Next, the lawyer informs him that his mother had listed him as the sole heir to her money. The lawyer handed him a check for thousands of dollars and then leaves.

The man breaks down crying, realizing that his wish caused his mother's death. The family tried to console him, telling him it was just a coincidence. In his grief, he wished out loud to his wife that his mother was still alive and there with them so he could tell her how much he loved her.

In the middle of the night, a banging and scratching on their front door awakens the family. They hear a cracked voice calling out to the man, "Son, let me in. It's your mother." As the man raced to the door, his wife shouted for him to stop. She knew the mother had died and been buried for days. She would not be what he thought.

As he opened the door, he saw the decaying body of his dead mother, once more alive, standing before him. He screamed and quickly backed away. His wife ran and got the monkey's paw and pushing it into his hand, she told him to wish that he had never come across it. As he did, the front door slammed. And all returned to the way it had been before he was given the monkey's paw.

self. It creates pathways of wonder and it is the blueprint for what we create in our lives.

Adults often say, "You create your own reality." If that is true and I'm so magical and powerful, then why am I not rich or thin or famous or whatever? It is usually because we did not learn to make the wish properly.

What is often not told to us is that making the wish and controlling the wish are two different things. There will always be some things in life that magic will not change. We can not control everything in life. If we could, we would never grow or develop. But we can control more than what we imagine. Before performing the "Fire and Ice Exercise" in the last lesson, would you have believed that you could change your body's temperature or the temperature around you?

There's an old saying: "Wishing will not get the cows milked." In other words, just wanting something to be will not make it so. But there is a secret to magical wishing and a skill to making things happen within our life. If we learn how to **work** with the magic of believing properly, the wishes we make will be fulfilled more often than we can even imagine.

Making Things Happen

So how do we make our wishes come true?

Is there a magical process for this?

The answer is YES! The magic of making our wishes come true is called *manifestation*. Manifestation is the process of making things happen, of bringing them into being. The process is both a magical and a practical one, and it affects everything in physical life. In order to make things happen, in order for us to have our wish-making work, we have to understand some basics about energy.

Energy is both electrical and magnetic. We send out and draw energy to us by what we think, believe, and do. If we wish to draw energies to us, we must send out the right message so that what comes to us is what we truly wish. The process of manifestation helps with this.

If we wish to manifest anything, whether it's better health, more love, a new job, changes in our life, or anything else, we must put energy into that process from all levels of our being. We are not just physical. We are also emotional and mental, and because of this, we must put emotional and mental energy into this process as well.

MENTAL ENERGY

We begin with mental energy. We are mental beings, and if we wish to manifest something, we must put a mental energy into this magical process. We must imag ine and visualize what it is we wish as if it is already ours. We talked a great deal about this in Lesson 2 where we learned that our mind is a magic wand.

We must be specific about what we wish. Imagine whatever you wish to, picture it as if it is already yours, and visualize it in as much detail as possible. Think of it as if you are picking something out of a catalog. You have chosen an item and now you are placing an order for it.

EMOTIONAL ENERGY

Next we put in the emotional energy. We are also emotional beings, and if we want to make our wishes come true, we must put emotional energy into this process. Although we don't want to use the emotional energy of desire, which is simply wanting or craving something. Desire can actually hinder or block the process of having your wishes fulfilled.

If we think, "I really want that" or "I wish I had that now," there is an implied *but*:

> I really want that, BUT I can't have it.

> I wish I had that, BUT I don't.

The implied *but* blocks or hinders the fulfillment of the wish.

We must put into this magical process is the emotion of **anticipation**. We must anticipate that what we are imagining, the visualizing of it, is already on its way to us. It's as if we have placed that order from the catalog, and now we are waiting for the mailman to drop it off at our front door.

We have all had this emotion. Think back to one of your favorite holidays or birthdays as a young child. You knew you were going to get something. You didn't always know what it would be, but there was still an excitement. You anticipated a wonderful gift. This is the emotion we must try to generate. Visualize what you wish, clearly and completely,and then get excited about it. Anticipate its arrival!

PHYSICAL ENERGY

Even if we put mental and emotional energy into this process, we must not forget the physical. We are physical beings and so we must put a physical energy into the process as well. Look at it this way. Imagine that we wish to have a new job. We begin by visualizing it in as much detail as possible. We picture all of the wonderful things that are ours now because of this job.

Then we apply the emotional energy. We know the job is ours. We are excited about it. We know it is being offered; we know it is on its way. We are already celebrating its arrival in our life and all that we will have as a result of it.

But even if we have put forth the mental and emotional energy, if we do not do something in the physical to help bring it about, it will never manifest. It is the physical part of the process that grounds and releases the mental and emotional to work for us.

In other words, even if we have visualized our new job, even if we anticipate its arrival, we must still prepare for it. We must prepare a resume, fill out applications, and do interviews. We must take appropriate physical actions to help make the job a reality or the job will never manifest. Our wish-making will come to nothing.

Two Secrets of Powerful Wish-Making

In more traditional metaphysics, there are two secrets to wish-making. They are called **The Law of Giving** and **The Law of Receiving**. Let me give you some examples of how I use these laws when making wishes.

THE LAW OF GIVING

Whenever I begin work to manifest my bigger wishes, one of the physical acts that I perform to empower and strengthen their fulfillment is through "random acts of kindness." This is a phrase for doing some act of kindness for someone that you may or may not know, completely spontaneously, and anonymously. Based upon the Law of Giving, **you must demonstrate that you are willing to give in order to receive what you wished for.**

When I am setting in motion a new project or working to manifest some hope, wish, or dream, I will per

Magicus Ridiculous
Ridiculous, strange, and amusing magical practices of the past

What Would You Wish For?

To Make Gold

Take the following ingredients: twenty parts of platinum, the same amount of silver, plus 240 parts of brass, and about 120 parts of nickel.

Melt these items separately in different crucibles. They are then combined together when in the molten condition. Then pour into moulds.

Sanskrit Magic Text

To Banish Pain:

On a paper hung around the neck, write the words:

An ant has no blood nor bile;
flee, uvula, lest a crab eat you.

Ancient Roman Formula

To Know of Things to Come

Mustella the wesell (weasel) is a beast sufficiently known. If the heart of this beast be eaten yet quaking, it maketh a man to know things to come.

Albertus Magus
(Medieval Magician)

For Love

Repeat three times while standing on the shore:

Waiting on Matsuo's shore this quiet evening for you who do not come,

I burn with longing, fierce as the fires of the salt-pans.

Japanese Spell

form a variety of anonymous, fun acts of generosity and kindness. Before crystals became very popular and few people had them, I would take small crystal stones, place them in envelopes, pick names from the phone book and mail them. I would attach a note that would say something very simple, such as "So that you can have a little more sparkle in your life ...A Friend."

If I am working on prosperity, I would take some one dollar bills and place them in envelopes with an anonymous note, such as "So that you will always know you will be blessed in life...A Friend." After I became published, I would often send copies of my books anonymously to people, sometimes gifting whole sets to spiritualist churches and metaphysical groups that were working to become established.

I always loved imagining what these people thought when they received their gifts. I could see them surprised and wondering, "Who sent this? And why? And what does it all mean?" They would be talking about it to their friends and their family. It would add wonder and mystery to their lives for days and would add a great deal of energy in turn to my own wish-making.

Part of what you can do also along this same line is to perform some volunteer or charity work when you start your wish-making. Help someone out without being asked. You do not have to commit to a great deal of time and effort, but do it willingly and joyfully, knowing that it is a way of helping others. And yes, you do help yourself in the same process.

Do not do it, though, with a grumbling attitude of "I have to do this or my wish won't be fulfilled." If you do, it will not work for you and may even backfire. You will have been better off not doing it at all.

The Law of Receiving

The other secret to good wish-making affects how and when the wish unfolds for us. This is called The Law of Receiving. **You must be willing to receive what you wish for and you must demonstrate that willingness to receive it.**

The Law of Receiving goes into effect from the moment we start to manifest anything and it always shows itself in our life within 24 hours. It starts small and subtle, growing bigger and more obvious. Within 24 hours of working to manifest our wishes, the universe begins to send us little gifts. It's a bit like a test to see how truly willing we are to receive the wish we are making. These gifts will come in many forms. They can be compliments, invitations, and offers out of the blue. They are little confirmations that things are starting.

We need to accept, to receive these little gifts, to start the stronger magnetic pull so that our bigger wishes will come to fulfillment. Our wishes are often blocked when we do not realize that this is happening and do not accept the little gifts. If we do not accept the little things, the universe will not send us the bigger things.

When you start to manifest a wish, pay close attention to invitations, gifts, and such that come your way.

Accept as many of them as you can and do not feel guilty about it. Guilt will block the process. It's a way of saying that you do not deserve to have your wishes fulfilled, and it will stop or hinder the fulfillment of your hope, wish, or dream.

There will be a time in which you can give back, so enjoy the receiving! Think of it like Christmas or a birthday, a time in which people give you gifts because it is a special day. Our wish-making is a special time, and if it is to succeed, we must treat it as such. Do you give back or refuse to accept your birthday or Christmas gifts?

Working with the Law of Receiving is what allows us to apply spiritual energies to our mental, emotional, and physical efforts to manifest our wishes. It is a way of saying that the spiritual part of you deserves and has the right to have your wishes fulfilled. As sons and daughters of the Divine, we are heir to all of the treasures of the Earth!

If someone pays
you a compliment,
accept it
graciously.

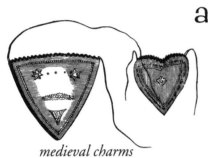

medieval charms

If someone
offers to give
you something,
accept it
joyfully.

If help is offered,
accept it gratefully.

THE MAKE-A-WISH GUIDE

On the following pages, you will see the **Make-a-Wish Guide** using the example of the wish to *find a good friend*. This guide shows you how to use all of the components we've talked about here which are needed to make your wishes come true. There are six steps.

1. Write the wish down.

2. Direct mental energy toward having the wish.

3. Put emotional energy into the process.

4. Invest physical energy into making the wish a reality.

5. Practice the Law of Giving.

6. Open to the Law of Receiving.

THE LAW OF GIVING. You must demonstrate that you are willing to give in order to receive what you wished for.

THE LAW OF RECEIVING. You must be willing to receive what you wish for and you must demonstrate that willingness to receive it.

Ted Andrews

Make-a-Wish

WISH	MENTAL ENERGY	EMOTIONAL ENERGY
Write down what you wish.	Direct mental energy toward having the wish come true.	Put emotional energy into the process.
Example *I wish to find a good friend.*	Decide how best to visualize the wish in your life.	Anticipate the fun and excitement of having a wish fulfilled.
	Visualize the ideal friend. List the ideal qualities and characteristics of this person.	Get excited and anticipate this friend coming into your life.
	• How would this person treat you?	Anticipate that this friend is already in your life. This person may just not be recognized yet by you.
	• How would you relate to this person?	
	• Imagine and visualize the kind of things you could share and enjoy together.	

Guide

PHYSICAL ENERGY

Invest physical energy into the wish-making process.

- Go to places you haven't been or spend time where others hang out.

- Make an effort to speak to people you wouldn't normally address, if only to say, "Hi, how are you?"

- Be physically accessible.

- Pay attention to those who speak to you or seem to pay more attention to you in the days ahead. (It is not unusual for invitations to come out of the blue. Even if they are invitations you would normally turn down, accept them. It will start the ball rolling.

LAW OF GIVING

Practice the Law of Giving. List the things you can do to help others.

If you are trying to bring a friend in your life, be friendly to others. Find someone who seems alone and or has few friends, and do something nice for that person.

Help someone out. Do a favor for someone out of the blue.

LAW OF RECEIVING

Open to the Law of Receiving. Pay attention to how people treat you.

If others offer help or assistance, accept it. If someone speaks (offers a greeting), answer with a smile.

Accept invitations. Pay attention to the little things others do around you.

Ted Andrews

Magical Mazes

SKILLS
DEVELOPED
- strengthens wish making
- creates opportunities to find solutions
- enhances psychic ability

Mazes are powerful tools for wish-making, problem solving, and psychic development. Mazes used in psychic development will be explored further in Volume III of this series, *Psychic Power.* As a practical wish-making tool, it is one of the best.

Mazes and labyrinths are found everywhere in the world. Fairy tales and myths speak of the hero's journey through a maze of difficulties to an eventual reward. All mazes have a starting point and finishing point. Sometimes the starting point is in the middle because in life we often are entangled and lost before we even realize it.

Begin to think of a maze as a magical tool. It is, in fact, one of the most beneficial and inexpensive tools you will find. For a small fee, you can purchase a book of mazes—a good supply of magical possibilities—at most stores that sell magazines. They teach us to use our imagination and focus on solutions, psychic insight, and success in endeavors.

For many people, the seeking of a treasure or the quest for a goal, whether it is manifesting a new job or finding a new love, can be incorporated into the solving of a maze. It releases the energy into our life that opens the doors to achieving the goal or finding the treasure.

Perhaps for you the making of a wish or the seeking of a dream is like having a prize dangling just beyond your reach. Working mazes in the proper way helps put the prize within your grasp. In time you will find many ways of adapting and using mazes for a great many magical benefits.

Visualize your maze as a symbol of a map to your treasure or wish. It can even be a reflection of a problem

that needs to be solved. We can have treasure maps or mazes for health, weight, beauty, money, relationships, creativity, and most any problem you want to solve. The maze will represent whatever you wish.

In our case, it will be a treasure of some sort. As you work the maze, know that you are winding your way to your treasure, to accomplishing your prize or goal. What you do on one level affects you on all levels. This will release powerful mental, emotional, *and* physical energy so the wish has greater potential to be fulfilled.

Be patient with your maze work. There will always be a solution or it's not really a maze. Keep your eye on the finish, on the treasure. Keep in mind while you work on it what it represents for you. Remember:

All energy follows thought.

You are turning the maze into a powerful tool of magic. And because you are actually working a maze, you are taking an appropriate physical action to help bring it about.

Magical Mazes (cont.)

WISH TIMES THREE

- *Set the mood.*

1. **Begin this exercise by selecting three mazes—ones that you have not worked.**

    At the finish point on each maze, write in what you are wishing for.

    Now someone always writes in the specific name of a secret love, thinking that this exercise will help make that person his or her girlfriend or boyfriend. It won't. Besides, it is wrong to try and manipulate and interfere with the free will of another, and it will come back on you in ways you will not like.

    If it is a new love that you seek, write down something like, "Someone who loves me and who is someone I can love in return." You might also want to provide some specific details as to the characteristics you'd like this person to have. This statement as is will easily fit your parents and grandparents, and that's probably not what you have in mind.

Magical Practice

2.   Label each maze with a different area of your life
     where your wish might come true.

     For example, you could put something like *work* on
     one maze, *school* on the second maze, and *play* on the
     third maze. This gives you a maze for three areas, three
     environments of your life where your wish could ber
     fulfilled. Remember that wishes can come true from
     anywhere.

3.   Take one of the mazes and work it from start to
     finish.

     By working the maze, you are releasing your wish to
     the invisible forces in your life.

4.   Take your Book of Enchantment and follow the
     steps in the "Make a Wish Guide" on pages 84-85.

THE MAGIC OF

Magical Mazes (cont.)

FOLLOW-UP

Perform this exercise three days in a row using one of the three mazes for each day.

Three is also a creative number, the birth number. Performing it with this rhythm creates the energy so that the treasures are more easily discovered or come into our life more quickly.

Repeat this exercise two more days in a row, using the other mazes. Then do not repeat it for at least one month. You will be amazed at what treasures unfold throughout the month.

Pay close attention to the Law of Receiving. This exercise always brings a variety of subtle gifts and offerings.

The Treasure Map

SKILLS
DEVELOPED

- strengthens intuition
- creates opportunities to recognize psychic insights
- invites prosperity and abundance into your life

We have all dreamed about finding a lost treasure. What an adventure that would be! Life is like this, but we often do not realize it. Most of the time, people go through life lost and never finding their way out or finding their treasures, as if in a daze. Once again you will be using mazes in this exercise.

- *Set the mood.*

1. Select a maze and set it in your lap for after the visualization.

2. Allow your eyes to close, and step through your doorway into your castle...

FINDING
YOUR WISH

You see yourself standing in the great library. As you walk slowly through the volumes of books, one falls from the shelf. You pick it up and as you start to slide it back onto the shelf, a thin piece of parchment falls out.

You pick it up, carefully unfold it, and you discover it is a map. As you gaze upon it, you realize it is a map of hidden passageways through your castle. It appears to lead outside to a secret garden to a tree. At the bottom of the tree on the map is a drawing of a sign that reads: "Here you will find your treasures!"

Your heart begins to beat faster. Could there really be hidden treasure? What could it be? Your mind races with the possibilities. You imagine what you hope it will be.

The map begins at the far end of the library. Against the back wall is a book shelf. The map depicts the third book on the left of the top shelf being pulled out. You reach up and as you pull this book out, the entire bookcase and wall swings, revealing a hidden passage behind it. You grin. Maybe there really is a treasure!

The passage behind the wall is dimly lit. You take a deep breath and step into it. The library shelves close behind you. The path seems to wind around and through the castle. You follow, unsure what you may find.

The passage twists and turns and you begin to lose your sense of location. You are no longer sure where you are at in the castle. And you begin to get nervous.

The passage widens and you can see markings on the walls. They are paintings and scripts you do not recognize. You are familiar with these images, symbols, and designs, but you don't understand them. Some are designs of spirals, reminding you of the mazes you puzzled over as a child, slowly drawing a line connecting one point to a treasure in the center or at the opposite end.

You continue forward, sometimes feeling as if you are walking in circles. At other times you feel you are simply doubling back. You are not sure what to think. You look to the map, but it seems to mock you as if to say, "Just follow the passage."

You continue forward, losing track of time and place. And then ahead of you is an opening. Bright sunlight fills it, and as you step through it, you find yourself in a magnificent orchard. The apple trees are in blossom and their fragrance dances over you, and you feel your heart beginning to sing. The grass is rich and green, the earth fertile beneath your feet.

As you look around, you see your castle in the distance. You are somewhere in one of your fertile valleys. You realize that you are still on a path, and you can see that the path spirals slowly around, lined with the magnificent fruit trees.

You follow the path, breathing deep the fragrance of the sweet blossoms. The sun is warm upon your body, and there is a sense of great joy. Slowly the path spirals in, and then before your eyes is the center—the heart of the orchard spiral.

Standing before you is the most beautiful apple tree you have ever seen. A soft breeze causes the blossoms to shimmer, and you find yourself enveloped in their fragrance. You feel so wonderful that you are sure this sight alone must be the treasure, for its beauty fills you. And just when you think it can get no better, there is a soft tinkling of chimes and from behind the apple tree appears a magnificent unicorn.

The light shimmers off of it, giving it a silvery glow. The

The Treasure Map (cont.)

alicorn, the horn in the middle of its head, shimmers with pearlescence. Its eyes fix you briefly, and again you feel your heart sing. It bows slightly, and in the blink of an eye, it disappears deep into the orchard.

You step forward and your hands brush the rich bark of this tree. You reach up and draw some of its blossoms down so you can inhale their fragrance. As you release the branch, you lower your eyes, and there at your feet is a small cedar chest.

A treasure chest!

Your heart pounds. You lean down, picking it up, and as you do, there is that same tinkling of chimes and a breeze swirls, and blossoms shower the orchard. You slowly lift the lid and see the treasures that will bless your life in the upcoming week. The air around you swirls with the pinkish white blossoms and their fragrance fills you—to heal and bless.

You do not know why, but you bow slightly to the tree and the spirit that you know must live within it. And you give thanks for the gift. You turn and you see the blossoms filling the orchard like the first snowfall of winter. You begin to walk back along the path, spiraling out from the orchard's heart center. You realize that you are working with the creative spiral of life. The going in and the bringing out. There is no doubt that each time you return, the wonders and treasures will grow greater.

Holding the cedar chest, you follow the path and soon find yourself at the passageway. You pause and look back toward the orchard, and standing at its edge is that same beautiful unicorn. Your heart fills with promise and then the unicorn is gone. But now you know where to seek it if you ever need its healing energy.

Ted Andrews

Magical Practice

You step into the passage. You are surprised to find that it is now brighter, and you walk faster, anxious to return home with your new treasure. Before long you are standing outside the library. The shelves open for you as you approach, and as you step through with treasure chest in hand, the image of the castle fade from the vision. But they do so only so their energies may be born into the outer life.

You find yourself back within your room. Your heart is still singing. The treasure has been brought from the inner to the outer. The magic is alive. You take a moment to enjoy the wonder and promise that touches every cell within you. And you prepare to open the treasure chest within your outer life....

3. **Now take the maze from your lap and work it from start to finish.**

   This grounds the energy of the meditation and helps set it in motion so that your treasures will unfold in your outer life. Save any mazes you work in your Book of Enchantment. When you finish the maze, take a moment and visualize your treasure chest opening and your wish appearing from within it.

THE MAGIC OF BELIEVING

The Treasure Map (cont.)

- *Perform a grounding ritual.*

  Take your Book of Enchantment and write in it what you felt and imagined while doing this exercise.

  List things that you can do to bring your wish about more quickly. Write out where the map led you and anything else that you discovered about that secret garden. Make a drawing of the map.

  Over the next week pay attention to invitations and unexpected help from others. These will be signs the magic is beginning to work. This exercise opens new learning opportunities which add to your life treasures.

Sailing Through Time

SKILLS DEVELOPED

- sets stage for time travel or past life exploration
- enhances healing or resolving issues of the past
- prepares us for exploring future possibilities
- strengthens lucid dreaming
- may stimulate out-of-body experiences

Did you ever wish you could change something you had done?

Or if you had the opportunity, would you do something over again?

Time is a dimension that only the best magicians are truly skilled at. Time travel takes great care, practice, and effort. This exercise will start you working with time.

Everything that has ever been felt or experienced has left an imprint upon a subtler dimension, usually referred to as the astral plane. The astral plane is a fluid, changeable realm of dreams and the imagination, but real. It is the place where energy forms and gathers before crystallizing and manifesting upon the physical plane of our lives. It is where our beliefs gather strength until their magic can become real within our daily lives.

When we are beginning to learn how to take better control of the element of time, we can use the symbols and images of ancient myths and tales. This meditation helps to strengthen your energies and develop the ability to access ancient times and places, real or mythical.

This exercise should not be performed too frequently. Once a month is all that is truly necessary. Remember, our focus should always be on our present life. If you find yourself running home to do a time exploration, you are using the exercise to escape and this will eventually create problems for you.

This exercise can trigger a replay of situations from your past. You may find people from your past popping back into your life. You may also find new people appearing who are very similar to those in your past. Situations with the same emotions and attitudes of the past may arise. This exercise provides you with the opportunity to handle these past situations differently, hopefully more successfully. By doing so, you free yourself of the past, sending a message out into the universe that you have learned your lesson. This eliminates karma.*

---

*Karma is a Sanskrit word, which means to do. Anything we do is a learning opportunity. With this exercise we learn to heal and we learn from past mistakes. The wish of a second chance comes to us.

Magical Practice

Uncontrolled fancy, letting our imagination go to extremes, is another possible problem with this exercise. If our lives are not glamorous, or perceived as being so, we may create imaginings from the past (past lives in particular) to make ourselves feel more important. If you find yourself rushing home to explore your past every night or find yourself becoming more dreamy and moody than usual, stop performing this exercise. This is

Fear and doubt close the doors to a magical life.

Practice believing and enchantment will fill your life.

Oracle at Delphi

Sailing Through Time (cont.)

a sign that you are becoming lost in an imaginary world rather than learning how to use your imagination more effectively. Our daily life should **never** suffer because of exploration and work with other dimensions.

In time, this exercise opens doors to the past which can be used to release emotions and mental attitudes you may have already come to terms with. It will also stir up some past life memories. These may show up in your dreams. Pay close attention to the emotions in your dreams for a week or two following this exercise. These may be emotions resurfacing from your past.

Apply common sense. I have met many people throughout the U.S. who have claimed to be a famous figure such as Merlin or Cleopatra in a previous life. I know of at least a half-dozen Merlins, a few King Arthurs, and about a dozen Cleopatras. I know this cannot be true…after all, I was Cleopatra—just kidding. Even if you get names, dates, and places, it does not prove that you actually lived that life.

With this exercise, we are again stretching our magical muscles. This exercise will develop concentration and creative visualization. It will help us to use our imagination in a manner that will help us see into other times, past and future. If the information gathered from doing this exercise helps us resolve a problem or to be more productive in our life, then it serves a purpose.

Magical Practice

THE GALLERY OF
YOUR LIFE

- *Set the mood.*

As you close your eyes, your room begins to disappear and you see yourself standing in the courtyard of your castle.

As you stand in the courtyard, the sun begins to set. You walk through an archway to stand along a railing overlooking the great cliffs and sea on one side of your castle. You breathe the salt air deeply from the warm breeze. From this railing is a path down to the shore where a tall ship is docked, waiting to sail. Out toward the horizon, you see a small island surrounded by a soft mist. From the shores below to that island you see many currents flowing back and forth.

You step from the railing to a rocky and narrow path. Slowly you descend to the shore. With each step you find yourself relaxing more deeply, a sense of lightness beginning to grow. It is a feeling of shedding a weight from your shoulders.

The sand on the bottom is soft and cushioning to your steps. You walk quickly to the dock and up the plank to board the tall ship. As you step upon the deck, the plank is lifted and the crew begins work to set sail. In a few minutes you are leaving the shore. The sails are raised and a soft breeze fills them. You take a seat on the deck and with your eyes upon the horizon, the crew goes about their work.

Sailing Through Time (cont.)

The ship moves smoothly through the waters. The gentle rolling motion is soothing, and your eyes close, relaxing. There is a soft bump and you open your eyes, startled. To your surprise, the ship has landed on the island. It's as if no time had even passed. You stand and look back. In the distance you see your castle standing high and strong upon distant cliffs.

As you step from the ship to the shore, you see a path before you and you begin following it. It rises gradually from the shore. With each step you find yourself lighter and freer. Each step up seems to shed the cares and tensions of the physical world. You are free and relaxed, completely at peace.

When you reach the top of the path, you are standing before a magnificent domed building. There is a soft violet mist dancing across the ground. You move forward and stand before a massive oaken door. The frame of the doorway is ornately carved. There is a relief carving of a vine that encircles the actual door. In the center is a carved symbol— ∞ —the symbol for infinity.

Above the door is a small plaque, engraved with your name. As you see it, you are amazed. You reach up to trace the letters with your hand, and as you do, the door slowly swings open, spilling out golden, crystalline light that surrounds you, pours through you, and then shines out from you. It is warm and nurturing…and it is strangely familiar.

You step through the doorway and into the great interior of this building. The door closes softly behind you and your eyes adjust to the soft light of the room. You look around and see artifacts from every corner of the world. Pictures, portraits, sculptures, clothing and weaponry. It is like a

Ted Andrews

Magical Practice

museum. Every time and locale seems to be represented here. Each has its own little cubicle, its area. Some of these seem familiar to you, while others are unrecognizable.

This is the Gallery of Your Life, with remnants from every lifetime and every memory that has helped to form you. It includes the real and the mythical, the ordinary and the fantastic—they have all helped to shape you. The cubicles closest to you are from special times and moments of your current life. Those farther away are from more distant times.

You step into a cubicle on your right and a smile spreads across your face. You remember these things! You pick up an article of clothing knowing you wore this when you were four or five. And there is what was once your favorite toy. You remember how you first got it and how you felt. My, how things have changed since then. The feelings of that time come flooding back.

There are photographs of people who were closest to you at that time. You pick one of them up and the person in the photo comes to life and greets you. You are so startled that you drop the photo. It becomes again just a two-dimensional picture. You realize you can talk to anyone from this time simply by picking up his or her photo.

On a shelf at the back of the cubicle is a book. Your eyes widen with glee. Even though it may not be the exact same book, it is still the one story from your childhood you always enjoyed most. Fairy tale, myth, bedtime story, whatever, it was always your favorite. Because it was your favorite, it still affects you and is a story that you can use to heal and manifest your own power and joy in life. You make

Sailing Through Time (cont.)

a mental note to find a new copy of it for yourself in the days ahead.

Without thinking, you hold the book close to your heart and make a wish about something you may want to change, relive, or feel again. It may be a wish for something new in your life or for something from the past. The book begins to vibrate in your hands. You hold it away from you and it begins to glow. The title of the story stands out brightly upon the cover as if in response to your wish. Then it fades and you place the book back on the shelf.

You step out of the cubicle and look at the wide expanse of cubicles forming this Gallery. So much to explore. So much to relive and remember!

It is then that the door through which you entered opens behind you. It is time to leave, but it is not forever. This is your Gallery. It is here for you to explore and open at any time. And each time hereafter you know that your visits will become easier and more fulfilling. You glance once more at the cubicle of your childhood, remembering the story, which contains much knowledge about the magic of your present life.

As you step through the door, it closes behind you, but you are filled with anticipation. These are times past, but only in the physical sense. They have left their imprints upon you and upon the world forever. As you walk back to the ship, it is comforting to know you can relive them and maybe change events that saddened you to create a different future. You step onto the ship and the crew sets sail for your castle.

You stand at the brow of the ship as it moves quickly through the waters. You stick your hands

Ted Andrews

Magical Practice

in your pockets and feel something at the bottom of one of them. You pull the object out and discover it is a medallion with the symbol of infinity on it. Your heart fills with a sense of hope and promise for the future.

Take a deep breath, feeling the room around you.

The ship docks at your shore and you quickly exit, climbing up the path to your castle. As you do, you realize that the past, the present, and the future are not really distances apart. When you reach the top, you look out across the sea to the island with your Gallery. You smile. So much to learn and explore!

You turn away and walk back into the castle courtyard. You stand in front of one of the doors. You take a deep breath and open the door. You step through with the symbol of infinity in your hand. You are back in your own room. Your breathe deeply, feeling yourself fully back—grounded, healed, and blessed.

- *Perform a grounding ritual.*

    Make a note of the book you held in your hands and the wish you made during the meditation.

    Take time at the end of the meditation to write down your feelings from the exercise in your Book of Enchantment.

Sailing Through Time (cont.)

Follow-up

See if you can find an actual copy of your book from the meditation and read the story.

Over the next week, make notes of any dreams of the past, people from the past that reappear, or replays of situations of the past. In time you will learn to control the time element even more.

A Variation

Another way to perform this exercise is to find a stairway to a secret cellar in your castle. As you descend, you grow lighter and lighter, and at the bottom you discover a room in which artifacts and such have been placed in storage very similar as to the Gallery in the above magical imagining.

SUGGESTIONS FOR PARENTS

➤ Make a wish list. Each of you write out "I wish…."
Make at least 10 wishes and share them with each
other.

Make a list of things you have always wanted to do
but were afraid of. Share them with each other.
Decide which ones are most possible and make plans
to explore them in the next week.

➤ Decide on "family treasures" (special trips, etc.) that
you could wish for and work toward together.

Use the treasure map exercise to help manifest these
treasures and plan random acts of kindness you can do
together to help bring it all about.

➤ Go to the library and get copies of your favorite story
or book from childhood. Trade and read each other's
book.

What do your stories say about each of you? Are there
similarities? Differences?

➤ Pick a time in the past in which there may have been some difficulties, and use the "Sailing Through Time" exercise to go back and try and understand it more, to change it.

Use this exercise to relive special, joyful moments you shared together.

➤ Spend one night per week reading to each other some of your favorite fairy tales. Some may claim this is childish and that bedtime stories are for babies, but the reading aloud of magical tales is a powerful process.

It may be uncomfortable and a little awkward at first, but the young and old alike enjoy storytelling. It will keep the magic strong, deepening the bonds, and developing the imagination.

Lesson 4

Stirring Your Psychic Powers

I know what you're thinking.

I had a hunch about that.

I should have listened to my inner voice.

Something just did not feel right.

I knew you were going to call.

Everyone is psychic. Everyone has the ability to see, hear, or feel on levels other than the ordinary. All of us have had some psychic experience, some hunch or insight that proved to be true whether, at the time, we trusted it or not.

Psychic ability is a learned skill just like any other. We all have the capability of working with our psychic ability, but it must be developed. The more we practice and use our psychic ability, the better we get at it.

Seven of the ten years I spent teaching school, I was a reading specialist working with high school students who either could not read at all or read so poorly they would have great difficulty finding a job. The most important thing I learned in those years was that anyone could learn to read. Some may pick it up a little more easily and more quickly than others, but anyone can

Magicus Ridiculous

Ridiculous, strange, and amusing
magical practices of the past

For Psychic Vision

Make a concoction of infant's fat, juice
of cowbane, aconite, cinquefoil,
deadly nightshade, soot.

Johannes Wierus
Sixteenth century demonographer

If anyone swallows the heart of a mole,
fresh from the body and still palpitat-
ing, he will receive the gift of divination and a foreknowledge of future
events.

Pliny the Elder
Natural History

learn to read. And even if we learn to read at only a very functional level, it will make our lives fuller and better.

Psychic ability is the same way. We can all develop our ability to tap into our intuition or to use our psychic or extra-sensory perceptions (ESP) to know things about ourselves, other people, places, or events, including perceptions about the spirit world. Even if we only learn to use our psychic abilities on a very basic level, our lives will be enhanced tremendously.

We have all had psychic experiences or will have them at some point. Young people have them more often and more vividly. Unfortunately, at some point they become impressed with the idea by adults that the experiences are "cute" and "imaginative" and hence somehow not real.

Perhaps you have already had many different kinds of out-of-the-ordinary experiences. You might have "seen" yourself in past lives and known your role as ancient individuals. As a child, you may have had what grown-ups called imaginary friends, but you knew they weren't truly imaginary. You might have travelled astrally, had lucid dreams, seen auras, and had clear psychic perceptions. These experiences are real, but they are often misunderstood.

Confusion usually arises because most people don't understand that the psychic potential is within all of us. The wonderful thing about living today is that we know more about the human mind and its possibilities than ever before. And that includes knowing more about our psychic potentials. In Volume III of this series, *Psychic Power*, we will explore this more completely, but for now remember:

 Everyone is psychic!

Most people think that you have to be special or gifted.

Wrong!

Some even think that you have to have been injured or experienced a major trauma to be psychic.

Wrong again!

Some people may tell you they are psychic because they developed their skills in a past life. This is probably true for most of us, but we still have to redevelop the skills in the present life. Usually those who make such statements are trying to impress others and making themselves out as something special. When we assume others are more special or more naturally gifted, we deny and give away our own power. We lower our self-esteem and we set ourselves up for failure.

Some individuals may be able to express and develop their psychic abilities more easily than others, but like any learned skill, it takes time and practice. If you want to learn to shoot foul shots in basketball, you must prac tice. The same is true for psychic power. The ability is there for all of us, but we must develop it with practice.

When we say
MAYBE

instead of
IMPOSSIBLE,

we open
ourselves to
great magic
and wonders!

Oracle
at Delphi

Magical Supplies

Every magician has tools to help him or her. In the beginning, when we are starting to develop our magical skills, these tools help us to accomplish our tasks more easily. They help us focus and direct the energies.

Two of the most beneficial tools are candles and fragrances. They raise our vibration, stimulate magical levels of consciousness, and are fun to use! And even though good magicians do not truly need them, they will often continue to use them because of the enjoyment and benefit they bring to the environment.

CANDLES

Fire has always been regarded as something mysterious. The way smoke melts into the air was often considered magical. Many traditions spoke, chanted, or sang prayers into the fire so as the smoke rose it would carry the prayers and requests to the gods.

For magical purposes, candles frequently serve as a symbol of the inner fires and can be used as an aid for meditation, for raising energy, for stimulating psychic ability, and for healing. Later in this chapter, you can practice a way to use candles to enhance your creative visualization and imagination with a magical practice called "Sacred Candle-Lighting."

Candles are also magnificent tools for using light and color in all aspects of our life. There are many candle meditations, techniques, and exercises to strengthen the body, mind, and spirit. The color of the candle and its vibrational energy is activated, released and amplified when lit. As the candle burns, its color frequency (energy) is released into the environment and into our aura creating changes and effects.

A study of colors will help you to decide which candles are most important for your own individual purposes. For instance, you can use colors to increase mental clarity (yellow) or stimulating spiritual and psychic perceptions (blue). Other colors are more effective for balancing (black and brown), protection (white), or for healing (violet or purple). See the table on page 122 for more information on candles and color.

FRAGRANCES

Fragrant oils and incense have an ancient history in magic, healing, and ritual. Most of the early incenses and oils were made from bark, herbs, flowers, and other plants. They are still powerful tools of the magician and healer.

Fragrances were used in the past to mask bad odors* and to pay homage to deities. Incense was a medium for prayer. As the smoke rose, so did the prayers and thoughts of the petitioner. Oils were used for anointing and blessing. Both have been used for healing and for

---

* You may have seen pictures of individuals in the Middle Ages with handkerchiefs hanging out of their sleeves or in their hands up close to their mouths as they spoke with others. These handkerchiefs were often sprinkled with oils to cover up the very bad breath from poor oral hygiene.

Ted Andrews

communicating with spirits. In every society, oils and fragrances have been used to counter the effects of disease and negativity.

Essential Oils

The study of fragrances and the use of aromatherapy in healing has become popular today. Fragrances are some of the most beautiful and effective means of changing vibrations—physical, emotional, mental, and spiritual.

Essential oils are made through a distilling process, and they can be quite potent and intoxicating. There are many ways to use essential oils, even wearing them like a perfume. Because of their potency though, they should always be diluted. Many essential oils are harsh and can burn or irritate the skin.

To affect our environment, essential oils can be used in a variety of ways. A drop or two within a small bowl of water will allow its fragrance to fill a room. They can be used in vaporizers and potpourri pots to fill a room with a particular fragrance. There are also expensive diffusers on the market, which will put the fragrance out into the air for extended periods of time.

We can also bathe in essential oils; a half a capful of oil per full tub of water is all that is needed. In this way, the fragrance can touch the whole body, affecting physically and spiritually, benefiting our auras throughout the day or night.

Incense

Incenses are commonly used in the form of joysticks and cones. The most common way to use them for cleansing or changing the energy of the aura or the environment is with *smudging*.

Smudging is a process to bless and purify a home, a person, or an environment. A smudge bundle, often herbs or incense, is lit. (The smudging process can also be done with a single joystick.) The lit bundle is breathed upon gently so the smoke rises. With the hands or feathers, the smoke is brushed over and around the person or the home, especially doorways and windows, to purify the area. The incense is often extinguished, or if further meditation or ritual is to be done, it can also be left to burn itself out.

Care must be taken with smudge sticks and other types of incense to make sure they are not placed near anything flammable. A good ceramic bowl with sand in it is very effective for smudge bundles (found at any New Age or metaphysical bookstore) but any appropriate holder to catch fallen ashes with work.

Incense and oils are beautiful tools that we can work with in a variety of ways. They lend themselves to individual adaptation. We can create our own personal anointing and blessing rituals by combining prayers, meditations, and various oils according to our purposes. Be creative in doing this. Trust your instincts.

Learning to use oils and incense is fun. We can become a bit of a scientist and at the same time help create an energy field around us that is strong and vibrant. We can use can use oils and incense to restore balance and health, to aid in protection, and to stimulate inner perceptions. The table on the opposite page contains a list of oils commonly available and used frequently for healing and blessing.

The Cinnamon Toothpick

As kids, my brothers and I would occasionally go to the store and buy a small bottle of cinnamon oil. We would then soak toothpicks in it and chew and suck on the cinnamon-flavored toothpicks throughout the day. Because cinnamon oil is very hot, it wasn't long before the toothpicks burned the inside of our mouths. We were also aware that the oil from the toothpicks would get on our fingers and so we were careful not to touch anything too sensitive.

On one of these occasions, my youngest brother was about five or six years old. He had been chewing on one of our cinnamon toothpicks when he had to go to the bathroom. My brothers and I, along with our mom and dad, were sitting in the living room, when a horrible scream comes from the bathroom.

My little brother comes running out of the bathroom, his pants down around his knees. His hands are cupped over his privates and tears were running down his face. He screamed over and over, "It burns! It burns!"

My brothers and I all looked at each other and we immediately cringed and grinned as we recognized "the cinnamon toothpick!" The oil from the toothpick had gotten onto his fingers. When he touched himself to go to the bathroom, the oil transferred to his....

Well, Mom jumped up, ran to help him, and washed the oil off of him. My brothers and I rolled on the floor laughing. We did feel sorry for him, but it was funny!

To this day, he usually gets as a present every Christmas a small bottle of cinnamon oil from one of his loving, older brothers.

Ted Andrews   121

 # Candle Colors

COLOR	USE
WHITE	purity; protection; amplifies the effects of other candles; awakens hope; can be used for any magical purpose
BLACK	powerful and protective; grounding and stabilizing; good for uncovering secrets.
BLUE	calming and healing; spiritual understanding; awakens intuition; used to bring in quick money.
BROWN	grounding and calming; wonderful to use in exercises for finding lost items.
GOLD	fulfillment of desires; mental clarity; prosperity; spiritual perceptions.
GREEN	growth and movement; awakening to nature spirits and Faerie Realm; youthfulness and fertility.
GRAY OR SILVER	wonderful for clarity in problems; awakens hope and possibilities; good in meditation to discover sources of trouble.
ORANGE	awakens joy and creativity; attracting to people, animals and other things you wish in life.
PINK	love and romance; success; awakens sense of honor; good for those developing psychic touch; visions of truth.
RED	passion and love; creative movement to attain ambitions; draws the energy of change; sexual energies.
VIOLET OR PURPLE	spirituality; healing; power and mastery; success in spiritual endeavors; transformations.
YELLOW	mental clarity; truth and wisdom; helps in making decisions; helps in learning.

 # Fragrances

Type	Benefit
APPLE BLOSSOM	promotes happiness; opens us to the Spirits of the Faerie Realm
BAYBERRY	eases fear and worries over money; calms emotions
CARNATION	powerfully healing; good energy pick-me-up; protects against oversensitivity to spirits
CINNAMON	magnifies the effects of other aromas; with sandalwood, deepens meditations; protection
EUCALYPTUS	calms emotions; stimulates psychic insight; eases nightmares
FRANKINCENSE	sacred; helps visions; enhances clearer psychic perceptions
GARDENIA	protects against psychic oversensitivity; calming, strengthens telepathy
HONEYSUCKLE	helps memory; awakens psychic abilities; helpful in resolving past issues
LAVENDER	magical and protective; helps open us to visionary states; helps in seeing spirit
LEMON	used by mediums for safe spirit contact, mental clarity
LILAC	healing; helps psychically attune to the Faerie Realm; physical vision of spirits
ROSE	sacred and healing; good for all purposes; assists in divination and psychic ability
SAGE	allows free flow from spiritual to physical; awakens psychic faculties
SANDALWOOD	powerfully healing; good for psychic touch; helps in work with spirits
WISTERIA	creative expression; belief in possibilities; spiritual perceptions

Ted Andrews

Sacred Candle-Lighting

**SKILLS
DEVELOPED**
- **enhances creative visualization and imagination**
- **promotes self-healing**
- **empowers the magical self**

The Magic of Believing is something that must be practiced. One of the easiest and most effective ways of practicing is by using this magical exercise to enhance your creative visualization and imagination. If you combine other magical practices with this one, you will increase the effects of all the others. This exercise more than any other one will be one that you will use throughout your magical life.

- *Set the mood.*

  Begin by choosing a candle. It can be of any color you wish. Place it in front of you. Eye level is fine, but have it where you will be able to see it.

- *Perform a progressive relaxation.*

1. **Take your match in hand and follow the scenario:**

   As you strike the match, focus on it as a symbolic act. You are giving birth to a living flame. You are participating in the ritual of lighting fires that has been performed throughout the ages, from hearthstones of primitive man to the great solar fires of the stars.

This match is part of a single living flame, with its original spark in the heart of the Divine. The power of this act rests solely with the fires of your own imagination and spirituality.

As the fire is struck, remember you are creating fire— causing light to shine where there was no light before. With this act, you bring warmth and change. This simple act brings healing to the soul for you are expressing the Divine within your environment. Your entire aura shines brighter, flaming strong.

As you take the flame to the candle, see the flame as the power of a great being or archangel or even the spirit of the Divine. It moves through space to bring light and life and new creation. Visualize the unlit candle as a dark planet or an unlit solar system, or even an uncreated soul awaiting the touch of the Creator to bring its flame to life.

2. **Extinguish the candle, feeling yourself empowered.**

Do not use the breath to extinguish the flame for breath is also creative. The creative should never be used to extinguish something else that is creative.

• *Perform a grounding ritual.*

The candle lighting should be a prelude to your actual meditation and the extinguishing should be the last act of the meditation. It allows all to return to rest and recuperation.

Ted Andrews 125

Magical Practice

Using a Psychic Pendulum

SKILLS
DEVELOPED
- **increases intuition**
- **promotes psychic abilities**

Pendulums are wonderfully simple and effective tools for learning to tap and hear the inner magical and psychic parts of us. They are one of the best psychic development tools around.

A pendulum helps us to tap the magical part of our mind—the subconscious—for psychic perceptions. When we ask the psychic part of our subconscious mind for answers, it uses an electrical signal to send the answers to us through the nervous system of our body.

This electrical signal travels through your nervous system, like your phone line, to send the message. These electrical responses cause involuntary muscle movements, a bit like your phone ringing, something you have no control over.

Using the pendulum like a phone, we can hear the answers more clearly. The involuntary muscle responses cause the pendulum to swing, giving us our answer.

Using a pendulum, we have picked up "the phone" and listened for the answer.

Learning to use the pendulum in this manner is simple. The first step is making the pendulum. The second is learning the language of the pendulum. The third step is connecting the pendulum to the psychic mind.

Making Psychic Pendulums

Making the pendulum is simple, and it can be done with objects found around the house. In time you will find it beneficial to have several kinds. Buttons, rings, and crystals are wonderful to use. They work best if they are balanced and have a little weight to them.

Ring Pendulum

They can be hung, tied, glued, or attached in some way to a thread, string, or chain about 12 inches long. A small necklace is quite good. I often wear a necklace with a pendant to use as a pendulum so I always have a tool with me if I need it.

Crystal Pendulum

Learning the Language of Pendulums

Learning to use the pendulum is easy. Begin by getting used to the feel of it. Take a seat where you can rest your elbow on a flat surface. Hold the end of the chain with the thumb and index finger.

Cross Pendulum

Magical Practice

Let the pendant end of the pendulum hang free for a minute or two.

Now circle the pendulum gently in a clockwise direction. Then let it come to rest. Repeat this again several times, both clockwise and counterclockwise. Yes, you are making it move, but you are just getting used to the feel of it at this point.

Now let it become still once more. Mentally visualize the thought, "swing clockwise." As you do, imagine this thought running down your arm to your hands and into the chain and to the end of the pendulum. When it begins to swing, mentally project the thought, "stop" and visualize it coming to rest. Now try the same thing in a counterclockwise direction. Don't be discouraged if it doesn't happen immediately. Remember that you are practicing and developing a new skill. You are still connecting the phone lines.

The third step is to teach the pendulum and the psychic part of your mind how you want them to respond. You are programming the magical part of your mind how to speak to you so you can understand the pendulum's movement when you ask your magical mind a question. You are connecting the phone lines between the magical part of you and the outer ordinary part so that the two can communicate more clearly.

Using a Psychic Pendulum (cont.)

CONNECTING TO PSYCHIC MIND

1. **Draw the following diagram on a piece of paper.**

This is a simple way to determe and get *yes* and *no* answers to questions.

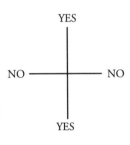

2. **Lay the paper flat on your desk or tabletop and hang the pendulum over the center.**

3. **Move the pendulum so it swings up and back in a vertical direction along the *yes* line.**

As you move the pendulum, say the following out loud:

> When I ask a question and the answer is YES, the pendulum will move vertically.

Let the pendulum come to rest. Repeat this same process three or four times.

Magical Practice

4. **Move the pendulum so it swings back and forth in a horizontal direction along the *no* line.**

    As you do this, say the following out loud:

    > When I ask a question and the answer is NO,
    > the pendulum will swing horizontally.

    Let the pendulum come to rest and repeat this process three or four times.

    If you prefer, you can also use clockwise and counter-clockwise circles for yes and no answers. Use the diagrams given below and program the pendulum in the same way as above.

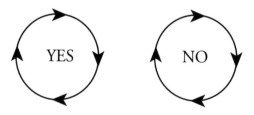

Using a Psychic Pendulum (cont.)

TESTING THE CONNECTION

1. **After programming the pendulum, test the process.**

    Ask yourself some yes and no questions, but this time do not move the pendulum yourself.

    Let the subconscious, the magical part of you give the answers. Use simple questions:

    Is my name ....?

    Do I have a brother?

    Do I have a sister?

    Am I _____ years old?

    Does _____ love me?

    (O.K., it's probably too early for that last one, but you should be getting the idea.)

2. **Practice this for about five to ten minutes everyday for a week.**

    You will be surprised at the results that you get in a short time. Keep in mind that this is not fool proof, but it is still an effective tool for getting the lines hooked up to your psychic faculties.

    In time you will learn to read subtleties in the way the pendulum moves. Fast and strong movements are clear, definite answers.

Ted Andrews 131

Magical Practice

3. **As you work to program your pendulum, prove to yourself that it will move without your physical help.**

   Dangle the pendulum over the diagrams and think *yes* or *no*. Allow your eyes to move in the direction. Continue this until the pendulum begins to move on its own.

To be effective with the pendulum, you must learn to relax. It is easy to manipulate it with what you want rather than what is. This is a problem everyone who works with psychic ability must control. Are we getting this answer because it is the true answer or because it is what we want? Only time and lots of practice will help you with this.

You must also learn to ask clear *yes* and *no* questions. The more specific your questions are, the better and more clear the answer will be. Notice the difference in what a *yes* answer could mean in the following questions:

Should I go to the dance tonight?

A question this general may not give either a yes or no answer. Or, the pendulum might very clearly say one or the other.

Using a Psychic Pendulum (cont.)

Will the dance be worthwhile for me?

In the sense that anything we do can be a learning experience and thus is worthwhile, but it wouldn't mean that it would be enjoyable.

Will I have fun at the dance?

You might have fun but it maybe only be for a small part of it.

As you learn to relax with the pendulum and work with it, you will find it a wonderful tool for getting clarity on issues. For instance, you can explore past lives by using a map and asking questions about previous lives in various countries. It is also a wonderful tool for finding lost objects, which we will explore in the next exercise. Don't be afraid to experiment, and have lots of fun with your psychic pendulum!

Finding the Lost

SKILLS
DEVELOPED

- awakens psychic ability
- sharpens inner perceptions
- enhances ability to locate lost items
- increases ability to work with pendulums

How often have we heard someone say or even said it ourselves, "I lost something, but I don't know where to find it?" Of course, if we knew where to find it or where to look, it would not really be lost.

Pendulums are wonderful tools for finding lost objects. The subconscious mind, that magical part of us, is aware of all that goes on around us. It registers everything. Because of this, we can use the pendulum to tap into the subconscious mind to bring information out.

The process is simple. If you are unsure where you last saw the object, make a list of every place you have been since the last time you saw it, This list could include places such as my home, the library, school, friend's house. If you suspect that what you lost is in the house somewhere, make a drawing of your house or us the sample house diagram on the opposite page.

- *Set the mood.*

  Set your list or map on the table in front of you.

  You may even want to use a candle. (Brown candles are good in meditation for finding lost objects. It is a color associated with St. Anthony, the patron saint of lost things.)

- *Perform a progressive relaxation.*

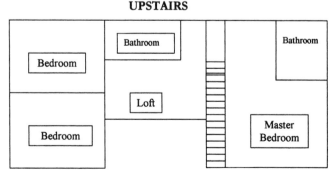

DOWNSTAIRS

UPSTAIRS

Magical Practice

Finding the Lost (cont.)

1. **Take out your pendulum and rest your elbow on the table, over the room on the map or one of the possible places.**

   Then begin asking the *yes* and *no* questions to narrow down the location:

   > Is it in the house?

   > Is it at school?

   > Is it at a friend's house?

   > Is it inside or outside?

   > Is it upstairs or downstairs?

2. **Move room by room and place by place.**

   Let the pendulum tell you *yes* or *no*.

   With practice you will be able to narrow down your search and successfully and quickly find things that you misplace.

- *Perform a grounding ritual.*

*Oracle
at Delphi*

I'm a great believer
in luck,
and I find that
the harder
I work,
the more
I have of it.

Thomas Jefferson

SUGGESTIONS
FOR PARENTS

➤ Take up candle-making together.

➤ Study and take a class on aromatherapy. Begin collecting and making your own oils and fragrances.

➤ Attend a psychic fair together and get a few mini-readings done.

Discuss what you experienced and how valid you thought it was with each other.

➤ Take a holistic healing class together. When I work with psychic development groups, I strongly encourage the students to also study healing.

Work with healing strengthens our intuition and psychic power and is one of the best psychic development methods.

It will also keep you more grounded and balanced. All the new psychic energy is less likely to create problems or disruptions.

➤ Create psychic games and contests. Keep it fun and enjoyable.

Whenever the phone rings, try and guess who is on the other line. Is it male? Female? What does he or she want? Do you know who it is specifically?

➤ Hide things from each other, and using a map of the house and your pendulums, practice finding them.

➤ Explore ways to use the pendulum to help you with diet, health, choices, and other decisions in your daily life.*

---

* You may find additional information about using pendulums for healing purposes in my book *How to Heal with Color: Balance Your Chakras.*

Lesson 5

Weaving a
Little Glamour

THE MAGIC OF BELIEVING

*If you could change yourself into anything,
    what would it be?*

What animal would you change yourself into?

What person?

*Can you imagine what it would truly be like
    to be that animal or person?*

In some of the ancient tales, we read about individuals who transform or shapeshift themselves into a beast. We are all familiar with the tales of the werewolf, but imagine if we could control our shapeshifting ability.

In those ancient times, there truly were certain individuals with the ability to change themselves into most anything at will. They could move between the physical and spiritual realms, adapting themselves and changing their energies according to their needs. They become whatever they dreamed of becoming and lived the Magic of Belief.

Good shapeshifters can draw upon their inner magic successfully for any situation that arises. Good shapeshifters relate to all people and adjust their behavior for school, home, work, or wherever. Good shapeshifters adapt to change.

Magicus Ridiculous

Ridiculous, strange, and amusing
magical practices of the past

To Become Invisible

This talisman and ring will make you invisible, even to spirits. You will be able to traverse the bosom of the seas, the bowels of the earth. Likewise you will be able to sweep through the air, nor will any human act be hidden from you. Say only: Benatir, Caracrau, dodos, Etimarmi.

The Black Hen (medieval grimoire)

Take the stone which is called Ophethalminus and wrap it in the leafe of the Laurell or Bay tree. And it is called lapis Obtelmicus whose colour is not named, for it is of many colours, and it is of such vertue, that it blindeth the sights of them that stand about. Constantinus carrying this in his hand, was made invisible therewith.

Albertus Magnus in *Magical Stones*

Imagine if we could shapeshift to accomplish our goals and achieve our dreams. Well, the truth is that all of us shapeshift. It is natural for us. Everyday, on some level, we all shapeshift to help us through the day. We learn early in life how and when to smile, when to be serious, or when to be studious. And most of us know how to present a particular image, but what we haven't learned is the next step.

It is something, though, that we can all do, and it begins by learning how to *weave a little glamour*. Glamour is an old term that applies to working your magic so that things appear to others as you wish them to. Weaving glamour is a form of shapeshifting.

When I was in school, I would raise my hand in a way that I would be noticed but not actually called upon to answer the question. I used a little glamour to give the appearance I knew the answer and most of the time it worked. The teacher would have the impression I was doing my work and was trying to participate in class. However, this is not the best use for this ability, but it is nothing new. Kids do this in school all of the time. Some are just more successful at it than others.

Good salespeople weave a little glamour around their products to make us want what they are trying to sell. TV commercials weave glamour through music and images to manipulate us to buy a certain brand name. They want us to feel that having a certain product will enhance our lives in some way we never thought of. They create a mood to influence us.

Weaving glamour is a process for bringing out the magical and more powerful aspects of ourselves to influence a situation. We draw upon our creative imagination to shape what is going on around us and to affect how people respond to us. We learn to tap into and project a particular energy around ourselves.

It is said that Merlin practiced shapeshifting continually throughout his life. When kings summoned him, he disguised himself as a poor shepherd, a woodcutter, or a peasant. He could present himself to others in any way he desired. People would believe he was just as he appeared. Because of this, Merlin was able to accomplish much within his life.

We are the shapeshifters of our life. We will all wear different masks at different times. The masks and forms we put on, though, should be ones that reflect the magic within us. When we learn to do this, we can recreate our life and how people respond to us. We can weave our life into anything we hope, wish, or dream.

Weaving the Glamour of Who You Are

Each of us is many things, and rarely will any two people ever see us exactly the same way. I am a teacher, a writer, a storyteller, and a husband. To many, though, I am also "the hawk man" because of my work with animals and birds of prey. I am all of these things and more. I have many parts to me, and the same is true for all of us. We play many roles in life.

Life brings many situations in which we have to use all aspects of ourselves. We become most magical when we recognize all of our aspects and the gifts each adds to our daily lives. Our task is to weave the inner magic into our outer life circumstances.

Where do we begin, though?

We begin by looking at ourselves a little differently than usual, noticing those magical parts of ourselves.

YOU ARE THE HERO

You are the HERO of your life. In stories and myths, the hero, or seeker, has many journeys and adventures into unknown territories, facing tests, and gaining magical helpers along the way. If the journey is successful, the hero is transformed with something to benefit the world around him or her. If the journey is unsuccessful, it must be undertaken again.

The hero learns by the decisions made and the results of those decisions. Making decisions and choices is what the hero must learn to do. In myths and stories, most problems arise when the hero hesitates or doesn't make decisions or choices. When we learn to make decisions, right or wrong, we are being the heroes of our own lives.

This doesn't mean you must make all decisions by yourself, but you still must learn to make them. If you

Our Magical Selves

I am the Hero of my life.
I make creative and responsible decisions.

Hero

Wise One

Warrior

Magician

I am the Warrior of my life.
I persist and endure to accomplish goals.

I am the Wise One in my life.
I succeed with wisdom and patience in all I do.

I am the Magician of my life.
I create and weave the magic to succeed.

wish to lead a creative life, you must make decisions about what you want to create. In other words, you have to realize that your decisions and your choices will affect you, your life, those who are closest to you, and in some ways, the world around you.

Learning to see yourself as the hero takes practice. One way to develop this ability is to take a minute or two the first thing every morning and the last thing every night and visualizing yourself as the hero of your life. Affirm it three times with some phrase, such as:

> I am the hero of my life. I make creative and responsible decisions!

To help us with this, there are three inner magical parts that everyone should learn to weave into his or her life for greater empowerment. (These are the three helpers most heroes encounter on their journey.) These inner magical aspects of you, the HERO, are the MAGICIAN, the WARRIOR, and the WISE ONE.

YOU ARE THE MAGICIAN

As the hero of our life, we each must become the MAGICIAN at times. This is what we are working on becoming with this book. Your hero's journey has brought you to this particular place in life. By the decisions you've made when doing the exercises in this book, you've shaped your life path and are now ready to weave magic around you.

The magician uses the power of the imagination and belief to help shape the events of life. We have spoken how the mind is like a magic wand and its greatest magic comes from our imagination.

Regardless where the hero's journey takes you, there will be opportunity to use your magic. Every aspect of life has its magic, including cooking, cleaning, writing, dancing, farming, or anything else that seems sort of ordinary. In other words, there are creative ways of working with all activities and endeavors in life.

The magician shows us how to project personal power, magnetism, and dynamic energy in all we do. This dynamic energy shows in our voice, posture, body language, and our aura. We project the image we wish others to see in order to accomplish what we wish.

This can be done for good or bad. Some people learn to use the magician in themselves to project confidence and then take advantage of others. A misuse of the magician energy is manipulation and deception for destructive purposes in life. Some use their magician to inspire and motivate others for constructive purposes.

We can awaken the magician by taking some time each day and visualizing ourselves as such. This is strengthened when we also affirm:

> I am the Magician of my life.

> I create and weave magic to succeed
> in my hero's journey.

You are the Warrior

At times, on our journey as the hero, we must also become the WARRIOR. The warrior teaches us endurance, persistence, and assertiveness. The warrior reminds us that without these qualities, the real magic is unlikely to happen.

Learning to assert ourselves is part of life. Knowing when to assert and how strongly to assert is sometimes difficult to determine. Often it is a trial and error process. Sometimes, in our enthusiasm, we can become too assertive, maybe even bullying.

As the hero of your life, you make decisions and choices that shape your life path. The magician, then, weaves the glamour and creativity to shape the success of the path. It is the job of the warrior to carry it all out.

The warrior is the one who gets things done. The warrior is the champion of your dreams. The warrior helps you fight the dragons in your life, not only those of fear and doubt, but also the difficulties and hindrances that arise. The warrior perseveres, doing what must be done

The warrior helps us with the discipline we need to pull all of our energies together. Without discipline, the goal at hand will not be accomplished. The warrior is the one who knows that there is work and effort in all endeavors. Through this magical part of us, we learn to be strong, focused, and persistent.

Oftentimes our warrior must go through trials and errors before we find a way to balance the energy.

Are we too aggressive or
not aggressive enough?

An unbalanced warrior will often be reflected within our life in one of two ways, as the bully or the wimp.

The warrior lives within each of us, but we must learn to trust in that strength and learn to express it properly. That takes time and practice, but we can help by taking time each day to see ourselves as a warrior and then affirming it through the following:

I am the Warrior of my life.

I persist and endure to accomplish goals.

YOU ARE THE WISE ONE

To help the hero, there is also a third aspect of ourselves, the WISE ONE. This is that part of us which always knows there is something to learn and something to teach in every life circumstance. It doesn't mean that the learning or teaching is easy, but the opportunity exists in all situations.

The hero in us chooses our life path. The magician within us weaves the glamour and creativity to shape the success. The warrior asserts and persists so the magic succeeds. The wise one helps us adapt it all to the circumstances that arise around us.

There are always things in life we cannot control. Because of this, things do not always work out the way we plan. We might have to adjust and adapt. The wise one helps us redirect our magic and persistence to accomplish and succeed in the best way possible, given the circumstances.

Wisdom is the ability to apply knowledge and understanding successfully. The wise one in us must be flexible and adaptable, with the ability to alter our course a bit to accomplish what we wish. Sometimes this means combining the faith of a child and the experience of an elder.

The wise one has a sense of where we are, whether or not we have bitten off more than we can chew, where we still have to go, and how best to get there. The wise one within us recognizes that there is often a larger rhythm and cycle at play and helps us to work with it. Things will happen in the time and manner that is best for us—if we allow it to. Through the wise one within us, we learn to express wisdom and patience.

It is through the wise one that we become a keeper of knowledge. We seek answers and we determine how to use them to accomplish our tasks. To help us with this, we should visualize ourselves daily as the wise one, strengthening the visualization through affirmation:

I am the Wise One in my life.

I succeed with wisdom and patience in all I do.

When we begin to believe once more in ourselves as the Hero of our life, the journey will become filled with wonder as the Magician, the Warrior, and the Wise One blossom within us.

*Oracle
at Delphi*

By the decisions
and choices
we make,

we shape
our path
in life.

Metamorphosis

SKILLS
DEVELOPED

- strengthens flexibility and control of energy
- promotes healing and transformation
- awakens creative imagination
- develops concentration and visualization
- enhances shapeshifting abilities
- encourages colorful dream activity

This is a wonderful exercise for stretching our magical muscles. It helps us develop the ability to shapeshift and weave glamour by enabling us to more easily access the magician, warrior, and wise one within us.

This very enjoyable exercise is also beneficial for anyone who is having trouble with nightmares—especially young children. With practice, you can see yourself flying off to dreamland as a magical butterfly. For parents who worry about neglecting their children while working on personal development exercises, this practice provides an excellent opportunity to invite them into your activity. Or the young person can invite their parents into his or her activities. They may initially be amused by it, but its effects too will surprise them.

THE MAGICAL BUTTERFLY

- *Set the mood.*
- *Perform a progressive relaxation.*

As you close your eyes, you begin to notice that you are not in total darkness. It is more of a gray. In your mind's eye, you see that you are sitting within a small spherical enclosure. It is formed of millions of thin threads, spiraling, and winding around you, giving you just enough room to stretch if you need to. It appears as if these threads have frozen into a silvery form. What light there is shines through them and casts a grayish, silver shimmer within the dome.

This is your cocoon. It is a cocoon from which you emerge each night. It is the cocoon of your life. Its only colors are grays and silvers. It is comfortable, but it is also limiting. The threads that form the sides of the cocoon are all ones you have sewn in your life. These threads have created a cocoon in which you can feel comfortable, safe, protected, and closed off. And yet through some of the threads come slivers of light from an outside world, shimmers that dance with new life. It makes you wonder what other beauties the outer world might hold.

You stand and move to a spot in the cocoon where a sliver of light from the outside sneaks through. You place your eye to it, squinting through the tiny opening. For an instant a rainbow of colors flashes in your eye. It is almost blinding in its intensity. The brilliance of the color is greater than you have ever imagined and it takes your breath away.

Ted Andrews

Magical Practice

You step back, filled with awe. You must see this other world as it truly is. You know that only within its light will you be able to see who you truly are.

You gently feel along the sides of the cocoon, searching for an opening. There are no doors and no windows. The sides do feel a bit rubbery, and as you push and feel, they give with your touch. With your hands, you slowly and gently separate the threads, stretching them like soft bands of elastic. You extend your hands and arms through the walls. The outer light touches them and a sense of freedom and power begins to fill you. Moving your arms, you stretch and wiggle, making the opening wider so you can squeeze your head and shoulders out as well. The sight is breathtaking and you freeze with wonder, half in and half out.

Before you is every color upon the planet and some you have never seen. There are shimmering emerald grasses, butted up against a vibrant blue sky. The earth is speckled with flowers and plants of every variety. There is a soft sound as if the plants and the air are singing in harmony to greet you.

Before you stretches an expanse of earth and sky so great that you wonder if you will ever be able to know it all. You pull yourself through and you lightly touch the earth. It sings as your feet brush its surface, and the sweet sound sends shivers of joy through your body.

You spin quickly about, trying to take in all of the sights at once. The spinning motion lifts you off your feet. You feel light and free, unbound to the earth. It is then that you notice you have wings—wings of rainbow light! Emerging from your cocoon has given you the opportunity to fly.

Metamorphosis (cont.)

The wings move with your thoughts, lifting you, lowering you. You begin to understand how magical a butterfly truly is. You fly slowly over the landscape, hovering about flowers and trees. Occasionally you light upon the flowers and plants, and this touching sends forth their songs into the air about you.

There is so much to see and learn. There is so much nectar to be savored, nectar that has always been present but usually ignored. You are filled with a desire to share this nectar—this world—with others. Will they believe? Will others be able to see that there is a magical butterfly within each of us, waiting to emerge?

You know you must take some of that nectar of light and creativity back with you. As your own life becomes filled with more color, others will notice and ask. But each of us must seek it out for ourselves. To simply tell others will never do. It is only when others are able to see the effects within your own life that their desire will grow and they will be able to add color to their own lives. Then it can be shared. When the desire is great enough—when there is the beginning of belief in new possibilities—the butterfly will emerge from the cocoon.

You look about the field of flowers. You choose one in the center of the field. It is a flower that has a special radiance for you at this time. Each flower is special. Each flower has its own unique qualities, energies, messages, and special gift. You float softly above it and then settle gently on the outer edges of its petals. It sings to you at your touch. The sound carries through your ears and into every cell within your body, caressing your cells with joy.

In the heart of the flower is its sweet nectar. You cup your hands and sample its fragrant elixir. Your head spins with

Magical Practice

a dizzying effect. You are filled with great joy. The flower has now become a part of you and you have become a part of it. You share its energy. It is a gift to take back with you. It may inspire creativity, intuition, prosperity, healing, or any number of possibilities. Each flower is different. Each is a gift, and there are thousands and thousands of flowers to sample.

You bow softly to the flower in gratitude. You rise up and float gently back to your cocoon. The sunlight shimmers, a rainbow prism reflecting off its surface. You spread the threads and enter, going back into your cocoon. You notice it is a little brighter inside now. The light shines and penetrates a little more strongly.

You know as you allow the magical butterfly within you to emerge more and more, the outer you and the inner, magical you will blend more and more. With time, the rainbows of one realm will become the rainbows of the other. Every rainbow has two ends, bridging and linking the two worlds together.

You settle into the center of the cocoon. The nectar is still sweet within your mouth. You know in the days ahead that it will affect your life, sweetening it in wonderful ways. You breathe deeply and allow the cocoon to fade from around you. Your own room and your physical surroundings begin to return.

You stretch a bit, feeling lighter and more blessed. You remember all that you experienced, and for a moment you can see your wings shimmering lightly around you.

Metamorphosis (cont.)

- *Perform a grounding ritual.*

  To ground the energy and make the magic of the exercise stronger, do some work with your Book of Enchantment.

  Research the flower that you touched. Make a drawing of it. Explore its magical, herbal, and other aspects. This will help you to understand how the flower's energy will touch your life in the days ahead. It is also a way of honoring the magical process that you have activated through the symbols and images of this exercise.

Magical Qualities of Flowers

ANGELICA	angel contact, intuition
BASIL	dragon energy; protection
BLACK-EYED SUSAN	helps us during changes
BUTTERCUP	compassion; healing
CARNATION	restores love of self; healing
CHRYSANTHEMUM	vitality and healing expressions
CLOVER	links to Faerie Realm; clairvoyance
COLEUS	open new spiritual paths; Arthurian legend
DAFFODIL	realize our inner beauty; deeper meditation
DAISY	inner strength; opens us to Nature Spirits
GARDENIA	open to telepathy; feelings of peace
GERANIUM	sense of happiness; strengthens aura
HEATHER	greater self-expression; good for shyness
HONEYSUCKLE	aromatherapy; overcoming the past
HYACINTH	restores belief in possibilities; assuages grief
IRIS	psychic purity; energies of rainbow; peace
JASMINE	prophetic dreams; mental clarity
ORCHID	sexual energy; creatures of Faerie Realm
PHLOX	spirit guardians; awakens artistic energies
ROSE	renews love; angelic contact; time exploration
ROSEMARY	fights black magic, hatred; astral projection
SAGE	slows aging; mediumship; ancient wisdom
SNAPDRAGON	protective dragon energies; hearing spirits
TULIP	greater trust; vision of the hidden
VIOLET	modesty; luck; psychic ability; Faerie Realm

Oracle at Delphi

Magic and miracles happen.
Life does work.
And enchantment can ber found everywhere...
if only we believe.

A Touch of Invisibility

SKILLS
DEVELOPED
- stills the mind
- increases the ability to weave glamour
- strengthens patience
- enhances invisibility

The idea of being invisible teases most people. There are so many things we could do. So much fun we could have. Everyone at some point has imagined what it would be like to be invisible.

There are many levels to becoming invisible and most of us have experienced some form of it. Remember the last time no one seemed to notice you? That's a form of invisibility. Remember the last time someone tripped over you, saying, "I'm sorry, I didn't see you there." That's a form of invisibility.

As a child, I was a bit sickly with very bad asthma, so I was often propped up in a chair in a corner of the room with the adults when there were gatherings and parties. I would become relatively invisible to them. In time, I began to enjoy those occasions because I would find out things about those present I would never have found out otherwise. When you are "not really there," people don't watch what they say.

When we can walk around without being seen and without anyone taking notice, whether we are physically visible or not, we are experiencing invisibility. When we do it at will, we are weaving a magical cloak of invisibility about ourselves.

There is a lot of confusion about the practice of invisibility, an aspect of shapeshifting and the weaving of glamour. Invisibility is a skill that takes much practice and requires learning to keep the mind still. Concentration is the art of holding a thought or image you have created without the mind wandering. With the following exercises you will lay a foundation for the developing your invisibility.

- *Set the mood.*

1. **Count slowly to ten, focusing only on one number at a time.**

    If you find your mind wandering, bring it back to the number.

2. **Practice being still, not moving, and only focusing on one thought or image (preferably yourself as being invisible) while in a group situation.**

    Parties, libraries, and other places people gather can be good places to practice this. Do this for longer and longer periods of time. Start with 30 seconds and then

Magical Practice

extend it. Visualize yourself as just part of the surroundings, like a piece of furniture.

3. **Practice standing against a wall and see yourself and
    your aura becoming part of the wall, just as if you
    were fading or melting into it.**

    Much of this ability is learning to control the aura, the
    energy surrounding the human body. You can learn to
    adjust its intensity so that you "blend in."

•   *Perform a grounding ritual.*

    Take your Book of Enchantment and write in what
    you feel and experience when you do these exercises.
    Keep track of how others respond.

    Above all else, make sure that you have fun with this.

A Touch of Invisibility (cont.)

THE FOX VARIATION

One of the best ways to develop invisibility is by working with "fox medicine" in Native American traditions. This is an animal that can be three feet from you in the wild and you will not know it is there. It knows how to be still and camouflaged. Working to blend in with your surroundings, to come and go unnoticed, is part of what fox medicine teaches.

Working to move silently without revealing your intentions is part of the art of invisibility. The fox uses its quiet and stillness for its invisibility. The next time you go to a party, take a seat on a couch or chair, and visualize yourself as a fox that blends in perfectly to the environment.

Imagine yourself taking on the pattern and colors of the couch or chair. Then sit quietly and watch how many people accidentally bump into you or even try to sit down on you because they did not "see you." You will be amazed. See yourself as blending into the gathering, melting into it. Do not be surprised as the night goes on that others will make such comments such as, when did you get here? How long have you been here? I didn't see you come in. When did you leave?

The more you work with fox medicine, the easier it becomes.

SUGGESTIONS FOR PARENTS

➤ List and share times and incidents when you each were the Hero, the Magician, the Wise One, and the Warrior.

What did you gain from those experiences?

➤ Everything in our life, everything we do or have, says something about us. It is a symbol. Our clothes, our hairstyle, our posture, and our trinkets all say something about us. With the young person in your life, list symbols of each other.

What do they say about each of you?

What does his or hers say?

What image are you projecting?

What image are you wanting to project and why?

How could you change the image?

➤ Write the story of your life. You are the main character.

> Where is the next chapter going?

> Are you more the Hero, the Magician, the Wise One, or the Warrior in life?

➤ Compare your life story to that of your favorite myth or fairy tale.

> Are there similarities?

> Differences?

➤ Practice being invisible together. Talk about times in which you both have felt invisible to others in your lives. You will be surprised how similar the situations will be.

Lesson 6

Creating the Magical Life

What if every day had something magical about it?

Wouldn't it be great to lead a "charmed" life?

What if there were special times to find magic?

Imagine if there were ways to uncover hidden,
        magical secrets?

There is no great secret to living a magical life. It is not done through spells or charms or incantations. To live a magical life, we must involve ourselves in life as creatively as possible and not hide from life or our responsibilities.

When we were small children, the world was full of possibilities. Each day offered new adventures and new wonders. Everything and everyone were special. Anything we could imagine was real, whether a ghost, a faerie, or time travel. We could be anything we wanted because then there were no limits or boundaries.

But as we grew older, fear and disbelief began to close the door to a magical life. For some, the streams grew silent and the winds no longer whispered and then one day, without our even realizing it happened, we could no longer see and feel the wonders around us. The enchantment of our lives had disappeared.

To live a magical life requires practice and watchfulness. We must learn to see ourselves as a walking, breathing, living force. We must feel every touch as a passing of power—to heal or hurt. We must hear every word as a stream of energy—to bless or curse. We must learn to see through the eyes of others—human, plant, and animal. Each breath should be a prayer and each step an adventure.

Creativity is natural for us and magic is an expression of our creativity. When we are not using our creativity, when we are not using our magic, we are not being who we could be. Unfortunately, we live in a society that has a small view of creativity. Some people see creativity as something that is cute, perhaps a hobby, but certainly nothing practical. For many, creativity is not a way of life.

Because of this, the focus in schools and in life is often one of seriousness and practicality. And these things must come first because some school administrators and teachers believe that it's the only way for students to learn how to be responsible. If this is true, why are so many people unhappy in what they are doing?

Why not be creative first?

Why not develop our magic first?

Then, when we develop skills for survival in the outer world, we will bring our greater creative and magical powers to those skills. This is not to say that we do not need to be practical. We can be creative as well as practical, but to be both takes a little more time and effort. The rewards, though, are well worth being magically creative in whatever we do.

There is magic in all things, whether you are trying to get a passing grade or cleaning up your room. When I am feeling disorganized, when I have a little creative block, when I can't quite get my thoughts together, or even when I am having trouble making a decision, I will clean something up that I have been ignoring. Sometimes I clean out a closet or I'll straighten out my office or rearrange it. I'll clean out the attic or reorganize my files.

Within a few days, the creative ideas start to flow strongly. I'll know what decision needs to be made or I begin to realize how best to accomplish a task. The cleaning and straightening is a magical act. What we do on one level affects us on other levels. As I clean up one area of my life, other areas straighten up as well.

This will work for you also. While you are cleaning up your room or straightening your closet, focus on a particular problem or area of your life you would like to have straightened out. Within a few days time, you will see a difference.

Before doing your math homework and solving the problems, take a moment to focus on a problem in another part of your life. Then proceed with the math. Within a few days time, an answer will present itself.

If you are writing something for your English class, see it as a magical act. Is there someone you have wanted to talk to or who you wished were talking to you? When we write, we communicate, opening the doors for more communication. In the following two or three days, pay attention to how many people speak to you, especially those who may not normally do so. You will be surprised. The greatest number of phone calls and letters I receive always come while I am in the midst of writing a book. (I'm magically open to communication.)

Everything we do is magical. The Zen Buddhists have a wonderful three-line poem:

I chop wood.
I carry water.
This is my magic.

They recognize we have already performed the greatest feat of magic—we are spiritual beings that have taken on a physical body. Because of this, everything we do in the physical is a magical act, whether it's chopping wood or writing the answer to an essay question. And if we can perform magic as magnificent as taking on a physical body, we should then be able to manifest a little better health, joy, prosperity, and love in our life as well.

The best way of keeping our magic strong is to be as creative as possible. Involve yourself in creative activities. But they must be fun. You must enjoy participating in them; otherwise, their magic is lost.

Activities to Awaken Our Magic

➤ **Take an art class.**

It doesn't matter whether you are good at drawing, painting, or other forms of artwork. If no one ever sees or appreciates your creations, it doesn't matter. Just have fun doing it. Art can be used for healing and psychic development.

➤ **Learn to play a musical instrument.**

Sound, music, and voice are some of the most powerful forms of magic and are wonderful tools for weaving glamour.

➤ **Study some form of healing.**

Self-healing develops your psychic ability and can keep you balanced as you open more and more to your magical self.

➤ **Learn a foreign language.**

Speaking certain words in a foreign tongue can be a wonderful magical tool. As you learn the language, see it as learning the ability to more fully understand the language of animals, plants, or even spirit.

➤ **Spend time in Nature.**

Nature is not only healing, but is also inspirational. It can open us to the Faerie Realm and other wonderful spirits in a balanced way.

➤ **Read myths, folk tales, and fairy tales.**

These stories remind us of possibilities. Remember there's a bit of magic spoken of in all of them.

Magic in the Seasons

There are rhythms to life that are stronger than our own. Most ancient and magical traditions realized this. They created ceremonies and rituals to tap into those rhythms to help strengthen their own magical endeavors. Some of the most powerful times of magical rhythms and possibilities occur around the times of the solstices and equinoxes. Every society taught the sacredness of the seasons. If we wish to truly unfold our magical selves and make them stronger, we need to work with the seasons as well. Every change of season brings a change of energy.

There are many ways to look at the year. We can look at it as beginning January 1 and ending December 31. We can look at it as following the planting season from spring to summer to autumn and to winter. The more magical and ancient traditions, though, worked with the seasonal magic differently.

YEAR OF THE SOUL

Autumn was the beginning of the year, followed by winter, spring, and then summer. This rhythm was called the *Year of the Soul* because it would bring out the magic of the soul, with the year becoming more powerful for the person.

The three days before the equinox and solstice, including the days themselves, are the time of change from one season to the next and called *The Holy Interval.* A time of the thinning of the veils between the physical and the spiritual world, it also stimulates a bridging between the outer and inner magical parts of us. At this time we can open up to our spirit guides more easily, we can strengthen our intuition, and we can manifest and make things happen more easily.Each season has its own qualities and characteristics. If we know what they are, then we can use them to make our own magical endeavors more powerful.

Fall

The fall season is the best time of year to initiate changes, the time of the hero starting the journey, the best time to shed the old and start the new. A time of sowing seeds to start anything new or for making new starts stronger and more likely to succeed. It is also the ideal time to sow the magical seeds for abundance. The seeds you sow in the autumn will come to fruition for you by the following autumn season.

Winter

Winter is one of the best times to tap your inner, magical self. The energy that is playing upon the earth during this season makes it easier to meditate and access our psychic ability. Dreams become more vibrant. Winter is a time though to slow down outer activity, but it is an ideal time to open to contact with spirits guides and angels. It is a strong time for the magician in us.

Spring

Spring comes in with an energy that can help us become more of the warrior. It is a time to assert our efforts and do what we have to do. Spring is a time to take things to the next step. Creative energies are strong and it's a great time to expand on those things we started in the autumn or take the time to help our magic along by doing what we can in the physical.

Summer

Summer is the culmination of the Year of the Soul, the time when we may have to adapt a bit to get the harvest—the results of what we are working for. It is a strong time for the wise one inside of us.

Summer is also a good season for psychic development and for connecting with spirit guides, especially those associated with Nature. Any work we do with relationships of any kind will be easier during this season.

The four seasons are calls throughout the year to come to the higher, more spiritual and magical, parts of us. They make it easier to express our magical energies and to strengthen our beliefs in new possibilities.

The Magical Seasons

Autumn Equinox

usually between
September 21st to 23rd

endings and beginnings; cleaning out
old and initiating new changes; harvest
and abundance

Spring Equinox

usually between
March 21st and 23rd

working with our creative fires; cleansing; expanding new endeavors;
greater self-expression; new opportunities; rebirth

Summer Solstice

usually between
June 21st and 23rd

abundance; love; hope; new relationships; or uncovering mysteries and
magic; contact with Nature spirits; or awakening psychic vision

Hero

Warrior

Wise One

Magician

Winter Solstice

usually between
December 21st and 23rd

slowing down outer activities and going
deeper when meditating; strong angel
contact; intuition; healing; new birth;
emotions and dreamwork

*Oracle
at Delphi*

We can starve
as much
from a lack
of wonder
as we can
from a lack
of food.

Creating the Magical Body

SKILLS
DEVELOPED

- **strengthens personal empowerment**
- **promotes healing and problem solving**
- **creates greater control in life**
- **promotes shapeshifting and out-of-body experiences**
- **awakens inner potentials**

One of the most important practices in magical believing is creating the magical body. To bring more magic into our lives, we must create our magical body. The magical body is a new, more conscious you. Through it we bring to life the unexpressed abilities within us. We awaken our higher and more powerful selves, bringing out the Hero, Magician, Warrior, and Wise One.

Through the process of creating a magical body, we awaken our hidden potentials and begin to manifest them in our life. For some people, the effects are subtle and take a little time to be seen. For others, it will be quite apparent. It happens differently for every individual.

Remember that through this exercise, you are creating a new you, not simply changing the old. We must keep this in mind, applying creative imagination to the ideal within us—physically, emotionally, mentally ,and spiritually.

The process is rather simple. Visualize exactly what it is you wish to be in as much detail as possible. Visualize yourself as if you have already accomplished it. Then do whatever is necessary in the physical to help it along. Act the way you imagine and believe yourself to be. When you change your beliefs, you change your world.

In the Book of Enchantment, begin by answering some questions to help you define your true magical self. Write out all of the answers, but leave space to add to them periodically. As you work on this exercise, your magical body will grow as you develop because writing out the answers helps to set the energy in motion that will help you to create your magical body. (Your answers can be both light-hearted and serious.)

Imagine the ideal you. Remember that if you can imagine it, then it can be.

> What is the most creative and brightest image of yourself that you can imagine?
>
> What is your ideal self truly like?
>
> What characteristics would you have?

Magical Practice

What would you most like to be able to do?

How would you like others to see you?

What abilities would you like to be able to express?

How would being this way change your life at home and school?

If you could demonstrate these abilities now, what are some ways that you could use them to benefit yourself and others?

How would you be able to help others without their knowing?

What would you be able to accomplish and how would you go about doing it?

What new possibilities would there be for you?

What would you change and how would you do it?

Once you have written out some kind of description of your magical self, prepare to do the exercise on the following pages.

Creating the Magical Body (cont.)

MEETING YOUR MAGICAL SELF

- *Set the mood.*

- *Perform a progressive elaxation.*

As you close your eyes, you look around you as you stand in the midst of the great hall. Already much of the castle is familiar and feeling more like your own special place. To your left is an arched door and you walk through it into an outer hallway. In this hallway is a great spiral staircase and you head toward it.

As you begin to climb, you find yourself relaxing more and more. With each step, you leave the worries, stresses, and fears of your everyday life behind. With each step you find yourself feeling free and light. Soft candles light the stairway, and as you climb higher, a soft golden mist swirls at your feet.

When you reach the top of the stairs, you find yourself in a long hallway with only one door in the center. At the opposite end of the hallway another spiral staircase descends. That gold mist swirls and shimmers, hiding the floor of the hallway. As you walk through this golden mist, causing more swirls, a soft tinkling of bells seems to issue forth from it, sending shivers of delight through your body.

You reach down and swirl the golden mist with your hands. You laugh at the wondrous colors and forms you stir within it.

Magical Practice

You straighten up and move to the door. It is large and wooden, carved with many strange symbols and letters. You reach out with your hand and trace some of them. As you do, the door slowly opens inward, as if inviting you in.

Your eyes widen as you step across the threshold. You are standing in a large, circular room that looks like an ancient magician's laboratory. Around the walls are shelves of ancient books, manuscripts, and scrolls. There are shelves of herbs, oils, and stones. Exotic plants grow in different parts of the room and seem to be watching you.

The ceiling is painted with a scene from the heavens and you gaze at the glistening stars. Then you realize that the stars are moving, the sky shifting. The ceiling is enchanted so if you wanted, you could trace the movements of the planets and stars in miniature. You watch the night sky shift.

You move further into the room and you find a large desk. Scrolls and parchment with written notes are scattered about the surface. Laying on top of them is your own Book of Enchantment! And you realize that this is your magic room!

As you smile, you continue to move about the room. Feeling even lighter and freer, you come to a full-length mirror. As you stand before it, there is no reflection. This puzzles you, but then a faint outline of an ancient face appears in the mirror. This startles you, and you take a step back. Then softly a voice speaks from that face in the mirror, "What is it you would see?"

Creating the Magical Body (cont.)

You hesitate, unsure, and then softly say, "I want to see me."

As you wish!" the voice replies and the mirror begins to be filled with misty clouds. As the clouds shift and part, you are amazed at the image that appears in the mirror. You see a magnificent person reflected there, shining with great light. You tilt your head trying to see it more clearly, and the mirrored image tilts also. It is only then that you realize the image in the mirror is the real you, the ideal you. The Magical you!

Your eyes are filled with wisdom. And there is a beauty, strength, and wiseness radiating from you. As you gaze in wonder at your true essence, flashes of your abilities and potentials appear around the outer edge of the mirror. So many possibilities!

As you look upon your true essence, the light grows stronger and to your amazement, your magical essence steps from the mirror and with your next breath melts into you. You close your eyes, feeling your true essence awakening. You see yourself stronger and more blessed. And with each breath you take, your magical essence grows stronger within you.

Your heart is filled with great hope. There is no doubt that in the days ahead this magical essence and all of its potentials will start awakening more fully. You offer a prayer of thanks of this reminder of who you truly are and for who you are becoming once more.

You step away from the mirror and look around this wonderful room. So much to learn and explore! You smile, empowered,

Ted Andrews

Magical Practice

freer, and more magical. You step toward the door and it opens. You step into the golden mist of the hallway and now it swirls up and around you like a golden garment of magic. The mist has recognized what has been awakened.

As you step down the stairs and the hallway disappears behind you, you breathe deeply, blessed. As you reach the bottom of the stairs, you find yourself back within your own room. You are balanced, healed, blessed, and empowered. You look down at yourself and stretch and see yourself shining brightly. Your magic is coming to life!

Creating the Magical Body (cont.)

- ***Perform a grounding ritual.***

  Take your Book of Enchantment and write what you felt and imagined while doing this exercise.

  Over the next week, pay attention to dreams and events around you as this exercise opens new learning and new fun. Pay close attention to how differently people seem to treat you.

The Sorcerer's Apprentice

SKILLS
DEVELOPED

- **opens contact with teachers**
- **creates new learning opportunities**
- **enhances self-awareness**
- **begins to awaken prophetic insight, especially through dreams**
- **encourages versatility and flexibility**

Stories, songs, and magic often went hand in hand in the ancient traditions. Storytelling was a means of passing on truths. Myths and tales served a variety of functions. They entertained. They enlightened. They educated. They even healed. Stories and myths cloak mysteries, teachings, and energies so that when we focus upon them in the right manner, they open to us.

Magical storeytelling offers wit and wisdom while inspiring our imagination and encouraging us to trust that the small things we do everyday are very important. To a young child, everything has life. Stones are alive. Streams speak a gurgling language. Animals think and everything has feelings.

Magical tales help us to find solutions to our problems. Bad luck must be dealt with; it cannot be ignored.

They remind us of our possibilities and teach us the responsibility for being productive in our life.

Because the images and symbols found within stories, myths, and tales resonate within us, they can be used for several kinds of magic. We will explore one kind of sympathetic magic here, meaning what we do on one level affects us on others. The images in the stories are ties to energies that can be released into our life. For this to work, we must place ourselves in the story scenario while meditating.

The tale which follows is an old one, adapted from several sources. It narrates a contest of shapeshifting that has been told in many ways in most parts of the world. It has been called the "Wizard Battle," "The Doctor and His Pupil," and even "The Sorcerer's Apprentice."

This magical tale is wonderful to use to practice placing yourself in different roles. Even though we may prefer to see ourselves as the hero, we all have qualities similar to the other characters as well, including the villains. Putting ourselves in their place will help us see our own weaknesses and how they affect others in our life.

This exercise always awakens self-awareness, psychic abilities (sometimes even prophecy), and new beginnings. It is usually followed within a short time by invitations and opportunities to study new things, especially those which seem fun to us.

Read through the story several times so you know the basic storyline. Don't worry if you forget parts. In time the story will change and adapt itself to you anyway.

Magical Practice

CHANGING
THE GUARD

- *Set the mood.*

- *Perform a progressive
  relaxation.*

*Allow your eyes to close, and imagine yourself standing outside
of your castle...*

*You are standing on the road outside of a castle that is remark-
ably like your own. You have a small pack upon your back. You see
yourself as a poor individual who is looking for work.*

*In your travels you have heard of a great wizard, a teacher
who needed a servant. You have been seeking out this wizard in
hopes that you can learn from him. You take a deep breath and
then you bang upon the castle gate. Before long a man appears at a
window above you and calls down to you. "What do you want?"*

*You reply, "I am looking for work, kind sir, and I heard you
were in need of a servant."*

"Do you know how to read?" asks the wizard.

*You hesitate, not sure what to answer. The question sounded a
bit like a test. "No," you lie, "But I am a quick learner, if you are
worried about being able to teach me."*

*The wizard answers, "I do not want anyone who can read, so I
will give you a try."*

*You enter through the castle gate. The wizard greets you from
the top of a tall stairwell and motions for you to follow him up.*

The Sorcerer's Apprentice (cont.)

You climb the stairs in silence. At the top, you enter a room, which looks like a mix between a laboratory and a library. In the center of the room is a pedestal upon which rests a large book.

"While I travel, I expect you to dust and clean this room daily and to protect its belongings, particularly this one book," he says, glaring down at you. You nod, looking at the book with curiosity.

Before long, the Wizard leaves for one of his long trips. He is no sooner out the door than you run to that one large book. You slowly open the leather bound volume and begin reading.

It is a book of magic! In it are all of the wonders of the universe. You begin studying it, memorizing it while the wizard is away. With each trip the wizard takes, you study voraciously. Always, though, you are careful never to let the wizard know what you are doing while he is away.

After three years, you have learned the entire book by heart, and when the wizard returns from his next trip, you tell him it is time for you to go. The next day you leave the castle and return to the home of your poor parents, anxious to try out some of your new knowledge.

There is to be a village fair within a few days, and on the eve, you speak to you father. "Tomorrow, you will find a magnificent steer in the stable. Take it to the fair and sell it, but make sure you return with its rope."

Your father gives you a funny look, but you say no more. The next morning the father is amazed to find the steer in the barn. He looks for you,

Magical Practice

but not finding you, he takes the steer to the fair. There he sells it for a good price.

On the way home your father hears footsteps behind him. He turns and sees you walking up the road with a big grin on your face. Your father questions you, but you tell him nothing. He does not know that you had turned yourself into the steer. After you had been sold, you turned yourself back at the very first opportunity.

Both you and your father delight in the money that was made. Each time money runs low in the house, you turn yourself into a steer, or a horse, or a fat pig to be sold by your father. After the sale, you turn yourself back.

What you did not know, though, was that to a master of magic like this wizard, any magic in the land would be recognized. And it is only a matter of time before the wizard for whom you worked knows that something is amiss in the land. It does not take him long to discover that it is you. He knows you must have read his great book, and so he begins to wait for his opportunity.

The next time your father brings you to the village to sell, the wizard recognizes him and he buys the horse your father is selling. He then takes your father to a pub and buys him many drinks. As your father drinks, he forgets about the rope by which he led the animals and which enables you to turn back to your normal form. Soon, your father passes out from too much drink. While your father is passed out, the wizard leads the horse to the blacksmith.

THE MAGIC OF BELIEVING

The Sorcerer's Apprentice (cont.)

"Give this horse a good shoeing," he orders, and with a smile he leaves for a time. You are beginning to panic, realizing what has happened. The idea of having horseshoes nailed to your feet is not very appealing.

Before the blacksmith begins his work, a small child comes along. As the horse you speak to the child, "Untie me!" The child is so startled, so afraid, that he does as you told him. No sooner is the horse untied than you transform yourself into a rabbit and dash off through the street.

The wizard sees this and he transforms himself into a hunting dog, giving chase. As the rabbit, you come to the pond and you turn yourself into a fish. The wizard turns himself into a man and returns to the town to buy the pond. Once he purchases the pond, he hires a group of men and orders them to catch all of the fish in the pond and clean them.

As the fish that is you is about to be cleaned, you turn yourself into a lark and quickly fly away. The wizard, though, transforms himself into a hawk and gives chase. Round and round you fly, darting and dodging in and out of trees, up and down hills. Still the hawk is on your tail.

Growing weary from the chase, you (as the lark) dive down the chimney of an old farmhouse. You quickly turn yourself into a grain of wheat and roll under the table. The wizard (as the hawk), though, is so close to you that he sees you change. He immediately turns himself into a rooster and begins pecking at the loose grains upon the floor.

Magical Practice

You wait until you are just about to be eaten and you transform yourself once more. This time you become a fox. And you eat the rooster.

When all is done, you turn yourself back to normal. And you realize that now with the wizard gone, his castle is yours. Soon you are comfortable in your castle, content to live out your days in wealth and wonder as you explore the magic of life.

You step through the gate of your castle and find yourself back within your room, where this adventure first began.

THE MAGIC OF BELIEVING

The Sorcerer's Apprentice (cont.)

- *Perform a grounding ritual.*

    Take your Book of Enchantment and write what you felt and imagined while doing this exercise.

    Over the next week pay attention to dreams and events around you as this exercise opens new learning and new fun.

The Magical Tree

SKILLS
DEVELOPED

- enhances the ability to see connections
- increases prosperity
- strengthens our potentials
- encourages fertility in life
- manifests change and growth
- opens doors to new opportunities

This exercise is a type of sympathetic magic, but it is much more. It has great symbolic significance and very powerful effects in our life over time. For those who may doubt that what we do on one level affects us on others, this exercise will demonstrate the reality of this magical principle.

The tree is an ancient symbol, representing things that grow, fertility, and life. To some, the tree is the world axis, and to others it is the world itself. A tree has its roots within the earth, and yet it reaches to the sky, so it is also a bridge between the heavens and the earth—the mediator between the magical world and our every-day existence.

The tree, as the Tree of Knowledge, has been associated with both Paradise and Hell. In Greek mythology, the Golden Fleece hung upon a tree. The Christian cross was originally a tree, and Buddha found enlightenment while sitting beneath one. Druids recognized the energies and spirits of trees, while the Norse honored Yggdrasil, the Tree of Life. Every civilization and tradition has its stories, myths, and legends of trees.

SYMBOLISM OF TREES

Trees bear fruit from which we gain nourishment. They provide shade and shelter. The wood is essential to the building of homes, and wood is also used for the making of paper, a source for communication and knowledge. The leaves of many trees fall in the autumn, only to re-emerge again in the spring, reflecting the continual change and growth, the dying only to be reborn. We rake the leaves in the autumn, gathering what has dropped to create mulch for future plantings. Trees also serve as barriers, often used as a windbreak or fence by farmers. They are boundaries, whether separating one piece of land from another or one world from another.

THE SPIRIT OF TREES

Trees have always been imbued with certain magical and spiritual attributes. The superstition of "knocking on wood" originated as a practice to ensure no spirits were in a tree before it was cut down and thus inadvertently upsetting them.

In German folklore, the *kobolde* were spirits inhabiting trees. When these trees were cut, a piece of the tree

Magical Qualities of Trees

Ash	might; immortality; source of life
Aspen	calms stress; communication; opens other planes
Apple	Faerie realm; healing; happiness; magical powers
Beech	awakens tolerance; contact with higher self
Birch	healing; staffs used to pass between planes
Cedar	protection; healing and calming to emotions
Cherry	insight, new awakenings; tree of the phoenix
Cypress	understanding of crisis; comfort in the home
Elder	burial rites mysteries; contact to Mother Goddess
Elm	strength when exhausted; intuition; fairy contact
Eucalyptus	protective; calming to emotions; vision of aura
Fig	freeing from past life issues; proper perspective
Hawthorn	fertility; creativity; sacred to the Fairies
Hazel	fruit, hidden wisdom; twigs powerful dowsing tools
Holly	awakens love; birth of Christ within; protection
Honeysuckle	learn from the past; psychic abilities; change
Lemon	cleansing to aura; invites protective spirits
Lilac	draws good spirits; activates kundalini; intellect
Maple	draws money and love; balances male and female
Magnolia	locating lost ideas or items; aligns heart and mind
Oak	strength, endurance; sacred tree of the Druids
Olive	peace and harmony; helps tap our inner guidance
Orange	astral projection; clarity of emotions
Peach	longevity; calms emotions; awakens artistic energies
Pine	salvation; calms emotions; link to ancient traditions
Sycamore	brings life, gifts; nourishment; beauty; links to Egypt
Walnut	hidden wisdom; transition power; freedom of spirit
Willow	healing; flexibility; seeing connections in events

The Magical Tree (cont.)

was carved into a figure so that the spirit would always have a place to live. These carvings were shut up in wooden boxes and brought inside of the house. Only the owner was permitted to open it, and if anyone else did, the result would be untold damage. Children were warned not to go near them, and jack-in-the-boxes were fashioned to scare kids and remind them not to touch the real boxes.

Most people are familiar with the family tree. This tree has its roots in our ancestors, both family and spiritual. All that we are lies in the roots of the tree, and thus all of our ancestry can be awakened through the tree. There are exercises we can do to reveal ancestors and past lives that have helped create and nurture the tree we are now.

PLANTING YOUR MAGICAL TREE

The process of awakening our own Magical Tree and all of its inherent energies begins with a simple and fully conscious planting of an actual tree. This can be a tree for the outdoors or one that can grow inside. It must be an actual tree though, and you must actually dig a hole, plant the tree and tend to it.

The kind of tree you choose is up to you. Each tree has its own energies and distinct properties. The table of tree characteristics on the facing page can assist you in your choice. Doing research on the tree, meditating

Magical Practice

upon it and deciding before purchasing, or transplanting the tree is a way of preparing our internal soil. Our consciousness is being readied for the awakening of the magical energies more fully.

By planting a tree, we perform a magical act of affirmation. We do not have to know all this tree will reflect. That will unfold as it grows and we nurture it, but we should be somewhat aware of its significance and our goals. Remember that most fruit trees have specific stages of growth and only bear fruit seasonally. It doesn't mean there is no growth at the other times, but it may be less visible, less tangible.

Do we want a fruit-bearing tree?

Do we wish to bear a lot of fruit in our own life?

THE MAGICAL TREE AND MAGICAL PRACTICE

The tree that we plant can be a wonderful way of empowering all of the exercises within this book. Before and after each exercise, we can take a few minutes and give conscious attention to the tree. Adding a little water before an exercise is a way of adding water to that aspect of our magic that we will stimulate through the exercise.

By taking a few minutes at the end of the exercise to reflect on the tree, what it represents and how much it

The Magical Tree (cont.)

has grown will strengthen the overall effect of this exercise. This will also enhance our concentration and focus. Just as a tree planted on a hillside can prevent soil from eroding, this simple gesture prevents the energy awakened by the exercise from eroding away or being dissipated.

Working the soil around your magical tree is a wonderful way to enforce the magic of "The Treasure Map" exercise in Lesson 3. This will anchor the energy of the exercise into the physical to help manifest it more quickly. You also affirm that you possess *the* magical tree where treasures can always be found.

At the end of the exercise, we can turn the soil around it or just place our hands within its dirt at its base. This is a way of grounding the energy we have accessed, and it helps to release that energy more tangibly and solidly within our physical life. Although it may seem silly to some or even mysterious to others, this is powerful and effective.

KEEPING YOUR TREE ALIVE

Inevitably there are some who will say, "I can't make anything grow. Every time I plant something, it dies!"

Magical Practice

The planting of the tree is a physical act to release change into our life. Death is always a companion to life, and it is change. It is part of the universal life cycle: life, death, and rebirth. If we are unable to deal with this aspect, we will have trouble with all aspects of life, magical or otherwise.

Difficulty in planting a tree that will live may be an indicator that the time is not right to work the tree you have chosen.

Are you choosing a tree based upon a magic that you desire but are not ready for?

Are you tending to the tree properly?

Magical practices, to be effective, must be performed consistently and responsibly.

On the other hand, we must keep in mind that the tree is an outer reflection of an inner energy. If the tree dies, it does not foretell our own physical death. Most often it reflects that an aspect of us that is no longer vital has changed. Maybe the chosen tree was not the best to start with. Some people choose a tree because of its extensive magical associations, but many trees are difficult to grow. Maybe the death of the tree only reflects attempts to undertake too much too soon.

With all work in magic, we must start simply. We must allow our magical tree (inner and outer) to grow

The Magical Tree (cont.)

at the rate that is best for it and for us. One of the qualities of all good magicians is patience. All magic has its own unique rhythm for each of us. Forcing growth impairs judgment.

Seeds need time to germinate, take root and then work their way up through the soil. Unfortunately, many people wish to have their psychic, magical, and spiritual development quick and easy.

With this exercise it is easy to assume that nothing is happening until we see the plant working its way out of the soil. Magical believing teaches us that things will happen in the time, manner, and means that is best for us if we allow it.

If your tree does die, give it back to the earth. Thank the universe for its presence within your life, if only for a short period. Then get another tree. And another, if necessary. If we wish to truly bridge and unfold our highest capabilities, we must persist. Everything we try and everything we grow within our life, successful or not, adds to our life experience and our magical, soul development.

 What we do on one level affects us on all other levels.

The Magical Tree (cont.)

1. **Study the characteristics associated with the different kinds of trees and select one that fits where you are in your life right now.**

   You have all of the time in the world to make this decision. You might find it easier to begin with the tree you have always felt closest to, your favorite.

   You could also go out into Nature and meditate on which tree might be best. Never choose a tree simply because you feel it may have more magical associations. These may not hold true or be effective for you.

   Think about your goals, both immediate and long range. Choose a tree that is appropriate for your goals.

2. **Plant the tree you choose where you will see it everyday, a visible reminder that as it grows and blossoms, so will our own inner tree.**

   This planting can be indoors or outdoors. If the tree is planted indoors, at some point you may wish to transplant it outdoors so it can grow freely.

   At that time, we may wish to choose another tree for indoors.

3. **The care of the tree is a potent part of this process.**

   As we prune and water this tree, you should be aware that you are also pruning and watering your own inner tree, enabling it to take stronger root so you can extend yourself to the heavens.

Suggestions for Parents

➤ Create some seasonal rituals you can do together. Plan them around the times of the equinoxes and solstices.

➤ Create a sacred garden area. For some, this may take the form of a fairy garden. For others, it may be a meditation area with plants. Plant a magical tree together.

➤ Take up artistic endeavors together. Remember that the idea is not whether you are good at it or not, but whether you have fun with it.

➤ Learn how to play a musical instrument. Sound and music are not only very magical, but also fun and creative activities. Anything fun and creative stirs up the inner magic.

➤ Craft magical items. Make power bracelets and necklaces using crystals. Create a meditation blanket or shawl and use it with every meditation so it can become infused with magical and healing energy.

➤ Make a magic wand or staff. Paint it and carve it with personal symbols.

➤ Explore. Take up a new study. Learn to heal. Have fun. Laugh. Do new things. Do old things in new ways.

Lesson 7

Precautions and Protections

There's no such thing.

Don't be silly.

You don't really believe that, do you?

Oh, grow up!

It's time you act a little more responsible.

How can I be so foolish as to believe all
    this nonsense?

How can I approach life from such a
    fanciful perspective?

I have had many people raise their eyebrows to my
approach to life. I am not saying we should believe in
anything and everything. I am only saying we need to
believe in something to keep a sense of wonder alive
within us.

We can either choose to believe or not believe. We
can either choose a life of wonder or a life of limitations.
Think back to something you used to believe in when
you were a young child. Faeries? Santa Claus? Ghosts?
Remember how you felt when someone convinced you

that these things weren't real. Some of life's sparkle was lost. Nothing was ever quite the same again.

Sometimes in life, it is more important to feel than it is to know. By remembering what we felt and believed as a child, we begin to rediscover the magic and wonders of life. I receive many letters from people exclaiming, "The most amazing thing happened! The things in your books worked!" Well, the amazing thing would be if they didn't. Life is supposed to work. Magic and miracles are supposed to happen.

Yes, trusting in our creative magic can be difficult. It means we must break old patterns. Even if these patterns are ones we don't like, most people are comfortable in them: "Better the devil we know than the one we don't."

To trust in our creative magic, we need a place of safety and for that reason, this series of books has suggestions for parents, so they can work with you and you can work with them. Together you find a safe place to unfold your magic.

 Believing is natural,

but it must be practiced!

Facing Our Monsters

There are three types of monsters to watch out for when we work with the magic of believing: Sirens, Gorgons, and Goblins.

SIRENS

The Sirens were creatures that lured sailors to their doom with their haunting song. The imagination is a powerful magical tool, but it must be controlled. The Sirens are related to uncontrolled fancy, wild, and over-active imaginings. Visions and insights can be nothing more than our own imaginings to make us feel good. They stroke our ego. They seduce the Magician in us. They reveal what we want to see, rather than what is or will be.

The Sirens often appear when people are dabbling or playing at being magical. False visions also happen when people try to do too much too soon. Remember, when we are really in touch with our magic, some things may emerge that make us feel a little uncomfortable to help us stretch ourselves just a little bit more. If we feel over-whelmed, then the Sirens have us and we need to surface from the magical realm and take a break from our explorations for a while.

The Sirens always surface when we are trying to get something for nothing. If we think that magic means not having to work, we will have problems or be lured into problem areas. Sirens are thoughts, imaginings, and people, which lead us away from common sense and balanced expressions of our magic. Remember that their haunting, seductive song led sailors to their doom.

Imagination is important to unfold our magical potentials, but it must be controlled. That takes time, practice, and constant observation. Working with someone you trust, such as a parent or friend who will be honest with you and have only your best interest at heart, is always helpful. Then you have feedback.

The more knowledge we have, the less trouble we will have with the Sirens. Studying, reading, and learning from a variety of teachers will help you ignore their song. Remembering that no one person has all the answers will help you as well.

GORGONS

In mythology, the Gorgons were three sisters with snakes for hair. One of them was Medusa. A single look from her or her sisters could turn a person into stone.

The Gorgons often appear in our life as family members and friends who do not want to see us change. They have frozen us into a role and they do not want to consider any other possibility for us. These people are sometimes like evil locksmiths who have locked us into a particular cell (a role) and they do not want to see us break out. From the Gorgons in our life, we often hear such phrases as:

Do you know how difficult that would be?

Why don't you be a little more responsible?

You are always doing that!

Why can't you be more like your brother or sister?

That's going to be way too difficult for you?

Do you know what other people are saying about you?

The Gorgons are best defeated through the Wise One or the Warrior within us. The Wise One has patience and can adapt and can see into the hearts of others. The Wise One knows if the thinking of the Gorgons in our life will change or not. All we can do is go on about our endeavors, living our magical life, working around these individuals.

The Warrior is the assertive part of us. We do not want to fight, but the Warrior knows how to persist. The best way to change people's opinion is by accomplishing what you set out to do, regardless of what they say or think. The Warrior in us has the ability to persist until we are successful.

Goblins

Goblins are mischievous creatures that are often depicted tormenting humans. These can be other people—or ourselves.

Other People

These are usually meddlesome people whose thoughts and opinions are likely to interfere with your pursuits. Goblins distract us. From them we often hear:

That's all you have time for anymore.

Is that all you care about?

It's not really going to change anything.

Friends and family can be goblins to us. Not everyone is going to applaud or support our efforts. They may be envious of our accomplishments or we may experience "unconscious interruptions" by them. In many situations, it isn't that they do not wish you to succeed, It is often a part of them that simply envies your ability to follow your heart.

Dealing with the thoughts and opinions of others is difficult. We want to be good friends, but first we have to be a good friend to ourselves. Imagine how much better you can be as a friend when you have awakened your magic.

Ourselves

One of the goblins we all must deal with is our own skepticism, which can surface quietly, whispering to us:

> That's impossible.
>
> That's too simple (or too difficult) to work.
>
> You're not gifted. How can you expect to do these things?

Hopefully, the exercises that you have completed in this book have helped to quiet these goblins. You should now at least be aware that you are more capable than you imagined.

There is an old adage that says, "There is strength in silence." In the beginning, to avoid interference with goblins outside of us, it is best to not talk too freely about what we are working on. It doesn't have to be a secret, but if you go to school bragging about how you are learning magic, you can get more than some funny looks. Some people will start to make fun of you and still others will unfortunately say things that can plant the seeds of doubt in your mind, and this can lead to your failure.

If someone asks, be honest and simple. Trust in the Wise One within you to adapt what you say and how you say it. If you have to, in time you will learn to weave a little glamour so other people will leave you alone. In that way, you can continue studying and growing without worrying about the goblins who do not want to see you succeed.

The MAGIC OF BELIEVING is actually very simple. Unfortunately, most people find it easier to believe in negative things rather than positive ones. How often do you hear people say, "I must have done something wrong or this would not have happened." Most people find it easier to believe something bad happened because of something they did wrong or because they didn't do something right.

If we believe in possibilities, we will find enchantment. If we believe, we will realize that there are still noble adventures in life. If we believe, we will hear the trees speak and the winds whisper. Every blade of grass and every flower will have a story to share with us. And in the blink of an eye, we will explore new worlds or fly among the stars. If only we believe.

*Oracle
at Delphi*

Our dreams are never lost, only forgotten. Believe once more and find your dreams!

Magical Practice

The Ancient Dream Guardians

SKILLS DEVELOPED

- opens us to surprise blessings
- presents opportunities for dreams to be fulfilled
- enhances lucid dreaming
- promotes healing of the past so magic can manifest more powerfully
- moves us out of limbo periods in our life
- encourages movement and growth
- awakens contact with spirit teachers

Of all the magical exercises that I have done and still do, this exercise is one of my favorites. I try to do it around the time of the full moon. If endeavors and things in my life are blocked, this exercise helps to release the energy for movement. It can awaken stronger contact with spirit teachers. This exercise is filled with images and symbols to awaken our inner self on many levels.

CHILD, MAIDEN, CRONE

- *Set the mood.*

- *Perform a progressive relaxation.*

A you close your eyes, your room disappears and you find yourself on a garden pathway outside of your castle. The grasses are soft and rich beneath your feet. The summer flowers are bright around you. The castle is behind you, and you are standing upon a path that leads down to a pool of clear water. At the far end of the pool is a waterfall. As you move toward it, you feel its spray, cool and misty on your face. As the falls splashes into the pool, any reflections are distorted. The sun is warm upon you as you stand next to the water.

You tilt your head, listening to the environment. You are surprised. There is no other sound other than your own breathing and the splashing of the waterfall. There is no other sound of life. This garden meadow looks pleasant enough, but where is all of the life? It appears to be all form and no substance.

As you stand next to the waterfall, you notice a small cave half concealed behind it. You step carefully behind the waterfall and into the inner darkness of the mouth of the cave. What little light there is comes through the opening by the waterfall. It shimmers through the splashing water, casting dancing shadows about the cave.

The air inside the cave is cool and damp. The floor is moist from the mist of the waterfall. The only sound is of the splashing until you step further into the cave and begin to detect a soft sound, a second splashing—only like waves against the shore.

Ted Andrews   217

Magical Practice

You move deeper into the cave, leaving the light of the entrance behind you. The ceiling begins to slope down, causing you to hunch. It is more difficult to see and you move more by feel than by sight. The sound of the waterfall becomes softer, fading, while the soft rolling sound of gentle waves against a shoreline becomes stronger. Still you move further into the cave. At the far end you discover a second opening. A pale light comes from the other side, illuminating this opening for you.

This opening has not been used in ages. It is thick with cobwebs, and you gingerly peel the silken threads back. You step through the opening and find yourself in an open place next to a large river. It is night time here, and only the light of a distant moon illuminates the area. Next to the water's edge is a small boat.

You step carefully down to the edge of the river. The water is black and it stills as you approach. The full moon reflects off of its surface, emphasizing the black depth, as if to tell you that these are the waters from the womb of life.

You look out across the river. A vague outline of an island is barely visible through the soft fog that surrounds it. It is then that you notice the man standing on the shore. Tall and broad, he looks at you with piercing eyes. He motions to the boat, inviting you silently. You hesitate, a little fearful of this strange figure. He gestures a second time. Still you hesitate.

He says to you, "We are never given hopes, wishes, or dreams without also being given opportunities to make them a reality."

The Ancient Dream Guardians (cont.)

His voice is soft, deep, and gentle. It touches a chord within you. You step forward and into the boat. The tall man steps in and stands in the back. With one of the oars, he pushes the boat from the shore. The trip is silent as he maneuvers the boat through the dark waters. Your only comfort is the soft reflection of the moon upon the water's surface.

Soon you move into the fog. It blocks your view of the shore and of the island. You are cloaked in it. Not even the moonlight penetrates. It is so thick you are not even sure you are moving. It is as if you are hanging in a cloud, stuck in limbo. You look toward your guide, but his face is stoic, showing no expression. He merely goes about the business of working the oars as if you are not even there.

Then you feel a soft bump, and you know you have reached the island. The guide motions for you to stand. As you do so, the fog begins to thin. He steps from the back of the boat and into the water. He wades to the shore and pulls the boat up onto the beach and then offers his assistance in stepping out onto the shore. It is then that you notice the medallion of wings that hangs around his neck. He nods in acknowledgment of your noticing, and then he steps back.

Before you is a path leading up a slight incline and out of the mist of the black river. As you climb to the top, you find yourself at the entrance to a large meadow. You see it is an open-air temple lit by torches and the full moon, which is now directly over-head.

In the center of this temple is an old stone altar. You walk closer, and upon the altar you see a mirror, a small bowl of

Magical Practice

water, and a medallion with wings, just as your guide had worn. Across the front of the altar, chiseled into the stone, are all of the phases of the moon.

From behind the altar, as if appearing from the shadows, step three women. One is a young child. The second is what appears to be her mother, and the third is an old woman. All three wear robes of gray. The old woman has an insignia upon her robe of the dark of the moon. The mother has one of the full moon, and the child has one of the new moon.

These are the creative forces of the earth and the moon. These are the feminine energies, the true Guardians of the Dreams. You are not sure how you know this, but you do. It is familiar, as if it is a replay of a long forgotten dream from childhood.

The child steps forward, lifts the mirror from the altar, and stands before you. She extends the mirror to you and says "When we first begin to open to new realms and new possibilities, we are all like children. These new realms and possibilities need to be nurtured and coaxed. The mirror is a tool that you can use to see how all life reflects itself within your life. It is a tool to help you see the night reflected within the day, the inner within the outer, the magical within you."

With these words, she places the mirror within your hand and melts into you. You feel her essence alive within you, a bridge to the magical energies of the universe coming to life within you like a child. You hold the mirror up and gaze at your reflection. Within your reflected image, you see the image of the child. She smiles at you,

The Ancient Dream Guardians (cont.)

and you cannot help but smile back, feeling a new sense of possibilities awakening.

The mother steps forward and raises the bowl of water from the altar. She holds it in front of you and you can see the moon reflected upon its surface. She says, "All cups, all bowls, all cauldrons contain birth-giving energies. From out of the cup of life comes the new. Out of the depths of the water comes new birth. As you learn to touch the subtle, magical areas of your being—as you learn to stir the magical waters within you—you shall be able to bring them out and drink of them fully within your day-to-day life."

She then places the bowl of water within your hands, and like the child, she melts into you and becomes a part of you. You realize the creative and magical exists in all life. You look into the water of the bowl and you see your reflection overshadowed by her. And you realize your abilities will allow you to give birth and re-create your life.

As you look up from the bowl, the old woman stands before you. Aged and wrinkled though she may be, she has a vitality about her that is eternal. Her eyes pierce deeply, seeing all within you and yet loving you regardless of it all. She holds in her hands a necklace of leather, with its medallion of silver wings.

She holds the medallion out to you, and you lean forward, lowering your head. She places the necklace and medallion about your neck and says, "There will come a time when these wings shall

Magical Practice

become wings of light. With them you shall be able to fly from one dimension to another, from night to day and back to night—all in the twinkling of an eye. These wings are the promise of the fulfillment of your dreams. It is the promise of magic born out of love through the expression of light."

In her face you see the young child. Then it shifts, becoming the mother, and then once again it shifts, returning to the face of the wise old woman. There is a sparkle of amusement in her eyes. She smiles warmly upon you, and gently cups your face in her hands. She places a kiss upon your brow and melts into you.

You raise your face to the night and to the moon above. You feel the ancient energies alive within you. You feel them awakening your magic and your dreams. You close your eyes and offer a silent prayer of thanks for the magic about to unfold within your life.

As if in response to your prayer, a beam of light issues forth from the moon above. It forms a silver, sparkling bridge of light back across the river. As you step upon this bridge of light to leave the ancient temple, a part of you remembers an old myth. It is a myth about walking upon the path of moonbeams, the path to your heart's desire.

You cross this bridge of light, and it empties you into the cave. The cobwebs are gone, and you hear the waterfall in the distance. You move quickly back through the cave and out from behind the waterfall. The sunlight greets you warmly and you step down to the pool of water.

You breathe deeply of the fresh air, and you feel as if the cobwebs have

The Ancient Dream Guardians (cont.)

cleared from your life—just as they seemed to disappear from the cave.

You pause, taking another deep breath, but your breath catches. A flock of birds fly overhead. A fish jumps in the pool beside you. You look across the meadow, and a deer walks serenely into the open. You smile. The garden meadow is alive! And there is life and sounds of life all around you now. Where there had been no signs of life, now they are everywhere.

And it is this thought that is strongest with you as you follow the path back to your castle. As you step into the castle, you walk to the nearest door. You breathe deeply, feeling the Ancient Guardians strong within you, and you step through the door back into your room where you are meditating. You breathe deeply, allowing the images to slowly disappear. You realize though that they fade from the inner world only so that they may now be born into the outer life.

- *Perform a grounding ritual.*

  To further enhance this exercise's effects, you should record your responses in your Book of Enchantment.

  Don't worry if the scenario did not follow exactly as it is written for you. As you grow in your own magic, the images and scenarios will unfold in ways that are unique to you.

Ted Andrews

Magical Practice

The Ancient Dream Guardians (cont.)

FOLLOW-UP

Pay close attention over the next week to your dreams, and record anything out of the ordinary in your Book of Enchantment.

It is not unusual for wonderful mirrors to come into a person's life after performing this exercise.

In Volume III, *Psychic Power*, you will learn how to perform mirror and crystal gazing.

The mirror can also be used to work with spirit guides which we will explore in Volume IV, *Spirits, Ghosts & Guardians.*

Suggestions
for Parents

➤ Try to identify the Sirens, Gorgons, and Goblins in your own life. How could you deal with them now?

➤ Make each other necklaces such as the one in the "Ancient Guardians" meditation.

➤ Find a mirror, cup, and cauldron that you can use in your sacred castle.

➤ What dream or wish would you like most to have fulfilled right now? (It must be for you and not a wish for someone else.)

astral plane	one of the dimension of dreams and things beyond the physical
aura	the energy field that surrounds all matter; around humans it is the electro-magnetic field
belief	a pattern of thougts that shape our behavior and life; confdence in the existence of something not readily seen or perceived; to know something truly exists, often without proof
clairaudience (clear hearing)	the hearing of spirits or voices that reveal information, usually refers to psychic perceptions through the sense of hearing, either an inner voice in one's own mind or a disembodied voice from someone in spirit form
clairvoyance (clear seeing)	the seeing of things, events, and people, including spirit; it can also refer to seeing the future or the past, usually a catchall word for psychic perceptions
	objective clairvoyance: the ability to see images and have perceptions outwardly with the physical eyes. Subjective clairvoyance: the ability to see images with the mind
clairsentience (clear feeling)	the ability to sense or feel things, events, and people, including spirits. It is often used to describe when someone has a "psychic feeling or hunch" (See psy-chometry.)

esp	extra-sensory perception; psychic and intuitive perceptions; knowing things beyond what is usually known by the five senses of sight, taste, touch, smell, and hearing
glamour	enchantment that attracts and influences
ground	to be balanced; eliminating "spacey or "out-of- sorts" type of feelings; to re-group and gather one's senses about himself or herself
imagination	the image-making faculty of the mind; it is used in all psychic and creative activities, including the receiving and sending of thoughts
intuition	psychic perceptions; the inner knowing and feeling
karma	to do; often thought of as cause and effect, but it is more what results from our life experiences. By choices we make and actions we take, certain events unfold for us
magic wisdom	the ability to make life work more effectively by applying natural and spiritual laws, by applying wisdom and natural abilities, such as clairvoyance and psychism
manifest	to make happen; to bring into being; to help bring about

occult	things that are hidden; usually associated with psychic mysteries
psychic	the ability to tap one's intuition or use ESP, clairvoyance or mental telepathy to know things about oneself, other people, places, or events including perceptions of the spirit world
psychometry	the ability to pick up the impressions from objects, places and people through touch and a heightened sense of feeling
shapeshifting	the ability to transform; to change one's shape energy and form
supernatural	beyond things that are natural; in reality things of the supernatural are things just misunderstood at this time. Psychic phenomena was once consider supernatural, but is no longer considered as such, but rather as natural to all people

Andrews, Ted. *Treasure of the Unicorn: The Return to the Sacred Quest.* Jackson, TN: Dragonhawk Publishing, 1996. [Cautionary Note: This book contains a small section of sexually descriptive content.]

A book as much about enchantment and believing and the wonders that can come from it as it is a book about unicorns and the Faerie Realm. You will believe once more.

Cameron, Julia. *The Artist's Way: A Spiritual Path to Higher Creativity.* New York: Jeremy Tarcher, 1992.

A tremendous book on awakening and manifesting your creativity. Inspirational, practical, and wonderfully empowering.

Gawain, Shakti. *Creative Visualization.* New York: Bantam, 1982.

Wonderful guide to techniques and applications of creative visualization and manifestation. It is good for beginners and a refreshing reminder for everyone of the power of visualization.

Nielson, Greg and Polansky, Joseph. *Pendulum Power.* New York: Warner Destiny Books, 1977.

Very practical guide on ways to make and use pendulums and dowsing as tools of our psychic development.

Weinstein, Marion. *Positive Magic.* Custer, WA: Phoenix Publishing, 1981.

A book to be read by anyone who wishes to explore the mystical or magical worlds. Whether Wiccan, occultist, shaman, or mysticæwhether novice or experiencedæall can find benefit from this book.

Any and all books of fairy tales and myths.

They are filled with magic and they keep a sense of adventure and wonder alive within us. They will always inspire, delight, and touch the child within. They remind us of possibilities.

THE MAGIC OF BELIEVING

- I -

imagination 14, 48-57, 110, 148
  exercises to enhance 124-125
incantations 4, 169
incense 119, 122-123
inner guidance 145
  use olive to tap 196
inner magic 145
inner mind 43
inner perceptions
  exercise to sharpen 134-136
inner potentials
  exercise to awaken 180-188
inner self 25
  good time to tap into (Winter) 176
inner mind to outer 96
insights, psychic 207
intuition 113, 178
  exercises to strenghten 92-97, 126-133, 134-136
  use blue candles to awaken 122
invisibility 142, 162-165
invisible forces 17

- J -

jack-in-the-box 195
Japanese spell 78
Jewish traditions 53
journey 145

- K -

karma 99
keepers of knowledge 151
kind acts 77
kundalini
  use lilac to activate 198

- L -

labryinths
  See mazes
Law of Giving 77-80, 83, 85
Law of Receiving 80-82, 83, 85, 91
learning opportunities
  exercise to create 186-192
  use yellow candles to strengthen 122
life path 147, 151, 153
limbo periods
  exercise to move us out of 216-224
links to the inner mind
  doorways 55-56
  pendulums 128-129
  secret passages 56
lost items
  exercise to find 134-136
  use brown candles in exercise 122
  use magnolia to locate 198
lost treasures
  exercise to find 92-97
love spell 78
lucid dreaming
  exercise to strengthen 98-106
luck 137, 160, 189

- M -

magic 170, 171-173
  activities to awaken 174
  defined 17
  inside of you 5
  most powerful of all 14-19
  rules for 20-23
  to succeed 146
  wand 35-38, 203
magical abilities
  test to determine 7-13

Ted Andrews

A Message from Lady Green

I am Queen of a band of Flower Faeries who live in southwestern Ohio. For many years, I've kept my faeries hidden from you, but now it is getting closer to the time when we are freer to show ourselves.

We're working with Pagyn Alexander to create a series of images for rubber stamp enthusiasts. If you'd like more information about our Lady Green rubber stamp collection, contact:

Whiskey Creek Art Stamps
P.O. Box 158
Hitterdal, MN 56552

218/962-3202

Young Person's School of Magic & Mystery
VOLUME II

Dreamtime Magic

by

Pagyn Alexander

In *Dreamtime Magic* you will learn how to understand and work with your dreams:

Hardbound

- to improve dream recall,

- to interpret dreams, and

- to control your dreams.

- to create dream doorways, and

224 pages

- to fight monsters under the bed.

You will also learn to use dreams for creative expression, self healing. and personal growth.

$18.95 USA

ISBN 1-888767-38-3

Coming Summer 2000

Young Person's School of Magic & Mystery
Volume III

Psychic Power

Hardbound

220 pages

$18.95 USA

ISBN 1-888767-40-5

by

Ted Andrews

In *Psychic Power*, you will awaken your psychic abilities and learn:

- to develop your psychic vision,

- to understand symbols,

- to know things through touch,

- to encourage telepathy with your pet,

- to make psychic potions and elixirs,

- to read the signs around you, and

- to divine the future.

Coming Fall of 2000

Also by
Ted Andrews

Psychic Protection

**Develop the
Tools for
Protection and Balance!**

At a time when so much information is available and so many present themselves as experts, a down-to-earth manual of psychic principles and common-sense practices has never been so needed. From one of today's most experienced and best teachers in the psychic and holistic fields comes a handbook for psychic self-defense that everyone can use.

This book provides practical scientific and spiritual tools for protecting our environment, our lives, and ourselves and will make the spiritual quest safer, more creative, and more fulfilling.

★ **Winner**
1999 Visionary Award* for
BEST SPIRITUALITY BOOK!

★ **Runner-Up**
1999 Visionary Award* for
BEST SELF-HELP BOOK!

358 pages   **$12.95 USA**

ISBN 1-888767-30-8

Available from
Dragonhawk Publishing
P.O. Box 1316
Jackson, TN 38302-1316

---

*   Visionary Awards presented by the Coalition of Visionary Retailers at the 1999 International New Age Trade Show.

Also by Ted Andrews

The Animal-Wise Tarot

The ANIMAL-WISE TAROT contains 78 full-color cards of actual animal photographs and a 248-page soft-cover text.

$34.95 USA

ISBN 1-888767-35-9

Available from
Dragonhawk Publishing
P.O. Box 1316
Jackson, TN 38302-1316

⭐ **Runner-Up**
1999 Visionary Award*
for BEST SPIRITUALITY
BOOK!

Discover the Language of Animals!

All traditions taught the significance of Nature—particularly of the animals crossing our paths, whether we are awake or dreaming. Use The Animal-Wise Tarot to develop your intuition, strengthen your connection to the animal world, and to find the answers to your most puzzling questions in life.

Whether an experienced tarot enthusiast, a shamanic practitioner, or a novice to psychic exploration, this tarot's clarity and ease of use will be a refreshing surprise. Anyone can use this tarot effectively from the moment it is opened and you will find yourself becoming truly animal-wise!

---

* Visionary Awards presented by the Coalition of Visionary Retailers at the 1999 nternational New Age Trade Show.

Ted Andrews is an internationally recognized author, storyteller, teacher, and mystic. A leader in the human potential, psychic, and metaphysical fields, he has written over 24 books which have been translated into many different languages.

Ted has been involved in the serious study of the esoteric and occult for more than 30 years, and he brings to the field a very extensive formal and informal education. A former public school teacher and counselor, he worked mostly with disadvantaged inner city youth. His innovative reading programs received both local and state recognition.

Ted also has many years of hands-on experience with wildlife rehabilitation, possessing state and federal permits to work with birds of prey. He has served as a trail guide and naturalist for children of all ages. He conducts animal education, storytelling programs, and metaphysical seminars throughout the U.S and Europe.

Called a true Renaissance man, Ted is schooled in music, hypnotherapy, accupressure, and other healing modalities. He has composed, performed, and produced the music for ten audiocassettes and he is a continuing student of ballet and kung fu.

Ted Andrews